CUTBANK

80

CutBank is published biannually at the University of Montana by graduate students in the Creative Writing Program. Publication is funded and supported by the Associated Students of Montana, the Pleiades Foundation, the Second Wind Reading Series, Humanities Montana, Tim O'Leary, Michelle Cardinal, William Kittredge, Annick Smith, Truman Capote Literary Trust, Sponsors of the Fall Writer's Opus, the Department of English, the Creative Writing Program, Judy Blunt, Karin Schalm, Michael Fitzgerald & Submittable, and our readers & donors.

Subscriptions are $15 per year + $3 for subscriptions outside of North America. Make checks payable to *CutBank* or shop online at www.cutbankonline.org/subscribe.

Our reading period is October 1 - February 15. Complete submission guidelines are available online.

All correspondence to:
CutBank
English Department, LA 133
University of Montana
Missoula, MT 59812

Printed by McNaughton & Gunn.

Copyright © 2014, issn: 0734-9963, isbn: 978-1-939717-08-5

CUTBANK EIGHTY

EDITOR-IN-CHIEF
Rachel Mindell

ONLINE EDITOR
Brendan Fitzgerald

ONLINE MANAGING EDITOR
Jeff Galius

ONLINE ADVISOR
Colin Post

SPECIAL PROJECTS EDITORS
Sarah Kahn
Allison Linville

ART EDITOR
Diana Xin

FICTION EDITORS
Brenden Olivas
Candie Sanderson
Asta So
Maud Streep

POETRY EDITORS
John Bennett
Kate DiNitto
Rachel Finkelstein
Philip Schaefer

NONFICTION EDITORS
Kim Bell
Kate Nitze

PUBLICATION INTERNS
Micah Fields
Sam Woods

READERS
Christopher Benz, Courtney Bird, Caylin Capra-Thomas,
Kimberly Covill, Sarah Dozer, Micah Fields, Brendan
Fitzgerald, Jeff Gailus, Sarah Kahn, Max Kaisler, Adam
Lambert, Allison Linville, Caitlin MacDougall, Daniel
Meyer, Alicia Mountain, Meghan O'Brien, Julia Ohman,
Bret Puryear, Michelle Seibert, Connor Willett, Rikka
Wommack, Sam Woods.

COVER
Anna Reeser, "A Turn in the Night."
Hardground and aquatint etching (Front).
Pen and ink, digital texture (Back).

CONTENTS

CHRISTINA OLSON

EATING KIT KATS DURING THE LAST HURRICANE, WE DECIDE TO SPLIT UP

We ignored the best reports,
didn't flood the bathtub
with clean water. And when
the storm did crack overhead,
we had only tiny candy bars,
pulled from the plastic head
of the pumpkin the treaters
never called for, our porch dark
and uninviting. We sat cross-legged
on the rug. The rain drowned
the frogs that used to keep us
awake. We were glad then
we had no children. We ached
for fiber, some green
and bright vegetable. But we
had only the candy. I said,
This is probably over, huh,
and you said, Please don't turn
this into some fucking movie.
I had meant only the storm.
Whoever calls rain cleansing
is a liar. Outside, something
cracked. It sounded like bone.

JASON GORDON

HOLDING MYSELF FOR RANSOM

I have no lungs

I breathe by
opening and
closing my fists

*

I can throw a pumpkin full of explosives
into the kitchen.

I can crush a cube of frozen paint thinner in my hand,
lay down on a domino the size of a mattress.

I can rip apart the garden shears
like a wishbone—

angels bouncing between spark plugs,
smoke doing its rain dance around the room:

no one will notice.
The sun is a junkie's eyeball and

rats stampede through the neighborhood.
I play chess against myself.

Every black pawn I take
I have to swallow.

*

It's the same every morning:
the house folds itself up like a map when I leave it,
static infecting the radio.

I wake the avocado not a real avocado
one from the garden where our ghosts hide.

I'm bored with my eyes,
I close them open them pull off my lips kiss my own nose,
the salad tongs in my hand.

JUSTIN CARROLL

PERU

The hardest part about vanishing was dealing with the daylight. The first day Cody and Liza left, Liza's father, her friends from the dorm, and her manager at Fire Tower Coffee started calling, texting. *Where are you?* They wanted to know. *Who took you?* Night made it easy to forget she was a daughter, a friend, an employee. At night, she only belonged to Cody, and in the darkness he felt like the only person she had ever known. They drank something or took something and her head was on his shoulder and he told stories most people would find terrible, sleazy, and all she could see was his face, hollowed out by the dark. Only his lips could make the skin on Liza's lower back surrender to goosebumps. But in the day, his lips felt like anyone else's—like Tanner from Intro to Sociology or that red-faced boy she met at a football game she didn't want to go to in the first place. In the day, she couldn't shake the image of Cody's wife and children wandering around Helena, looking for him—or her father, locked in the bathroom, ignoring his wife's knocking, drinking wine from the bottle and staring at his phone, begging it to show him an answer for why his daughter was gone. At night, Peru seemed as easy to get to as Miles City or Idaho Falls or Butte. In the day, she had to deal with the fact that they were in Crawford, Oklahoma, and out of money.

Now, Liza sat in the passenger seat of her '92 Nissan Sentra, a high school graduation present from her father last year. Next to her, Cody picked at his fingernails with a weed stem. He stared at the gas gauge, which had been blinking orange for the past twenty miles, as if he could will the needle back to a half tank. They were parked in front of a beige-bricked police station with an American flag wagging above it in the hot, stale air.

"All right," Cody said, turning toward her. "Go tell the person at the front desk that you're on your way to your mother's funeral, that you ran out of gas."

Since the air conditioning had quit somewhere in the yellowed nothingness of Kansas, they'd had to ride with the windows rolled down. There was an arch of dirt smudged across his forehead, and on his neck, near the long purplish scar he got from a car wreck back when he was Liza's age, a grayish leaf clung to his skin. Liza inspected the imperfections on his Nirvana shirt: toothpaste smeared near the shoulder, a brownish blood drop staining the blond of Kurt's stringy hair, the stretched and frayed neckline. Near Cody's left sleeve, she could see the blue tentacles of the octopus tattoo he did himself while he was in a group home. This was the one he hated, the one he always talked about getting covered up when he had enough money, but it was Liza's favorite. She loved how, when he turned his arm a certain way, it looked like a big, bumpy brain.

"Don't make it complicated," he instructed. "Your mother died. You're going to the funeral." Liza stared at the windshield. Above the wiper, a moth's wing waved at her. "It's gotta be your mother—no one gives a shit about fathers. Keep the story in the front of your mind, just in case they question some detail."

She wondered what it would be like to be on her way to her mother's funeral; Liza hadn't seen her mother in what? Eight years? Ten. Jesus, she thought, can't even remember. A splash of shame warmed her cheeks, but she shook it off. Her mother was the one who left.

Liza brushed off Cody's forehead with a McDonald's napkin, plucked off the leaf, flicked it out the window. "How'd you not notice that?"

"They'll have to help you." He squinted into the sun as he spoke. This made him look older—his features, she thought, were made to be scrutinized in moonlight or the merciful beam of streetlights, not bald, unforgiving sunlight. No, she corrected herself, this makes him look his age: thirty-six. "Every city's got an Emergency Assistance Fund."

"This isn't a city."

"You've got one, too." He reached over and pulled a twig

from her hair. His hand lingered for a moment. He ran his fingers down to her ear and squeezed it. He always told Liza he loved her ears. He lit a cigarette, handed it to her. "The smaller the better. Bigger places have so many goddamn resources it'd take us days to talk to the right person."

"How do you know every place has this?" Liza's phone vibrated in her pocket: Sara. *im borrrred. if anyone wants to go to canyon lake hit me up.*

"Your hair looks good right now," Cody said. "The wind's done wonders to it."

"I'm sure," she said. "Better than the salon."

"Trust me," he said. "All you need is a sad story and a valid driver's license."

She looked out the window at the station. The sky was an obnoxious sort of blue, the kind most people used to describe a beautiful day, but to Liza this kind, without any clouds, no hint of a change in weather coming, was oppressive.

"It'll be a piece of cake," he said. He put his hand on her thigh. "You'll have no problems—I got all the way to Ohio and back doing this trick."

Cody knew things most people could go their whole lives not knowing about. That Senator Burns has size six feet but wears size eight shoes, for instance. That most employers don't actually check if you have a college diploma before they hire you. She loved that about him. Everything he'd shared with her since the start of the summer interested her more than the things she'd learned in Macroeconomics, Freshmen Writing I & II, 19th Century American History—facts she studied for hours. Now, if she tried to focus on just one thing she'd been told by her professors last year, she came up with nothing.

She shook her head, shielded her eyes from the sun. She said, "I can't do it."

A little boy came out of a house across from the station eating a red Popsicle. He looked young, maybe eight or nine, Liza thought. The boy kept his head forward and held his hands out, careful not to stain his clothes. Liza turned and saw that Cody was watching; his mouth was now open, as if he wanted a bite of the Popsicle.

"Thinkin' about them?" Liza asked. She touched his hand. She hoped that he might say something here, might give her a reason why leaving with her in the middle of the night was more important than staying with his children, or at least staying in the same state as his children, or at least saying goodbye to them one last time.

"You have to do it," he said quickly. He took his hand away from her thigh, leaving a wet handprint on her shorts. "You have to. We're outta options."

"You do it."

"Might have a warrant."

He pulled himself out of the car, stretched. "I'm gonna walk 'round the corner, just in case they come out to make sure your tags aren't expired."

She stayed in the car; Cody walked around to her side and opened her door. "Let me borrow your phone. I'll see if my 401K's been processed yet. Plus, I got a friend in Broken Arrow who might be able to help us out."

Her phone vibrated—a text from her father. *ur friends tell me that ur safe, ur away with someone. Why won't u tell me urself?*

Cody took her face in his hands, kissed her forehead. "Once we get the money from my 401K, it'll be smooth sailing all the way to Peru. I promise."

The police station's tile floor was white and spiderwebbed with cracks. Posters lined the hallway endorsing wearing seatbelts, warning of the poisonous snakes native to Oklahoma. Close to the

Plexiglas window, behind which a red-headed woman sat in front of a computer, there was a corkboard tacked with photos of WANTED or MISSING people. When she was younger, before she hated her, Liza would ride her bike to the post office to look for her mother. She was only considered missing for three months, and Liza never saw her mother staring back at her among the grainy faces of the disappeared. Even so, she kept riding her bike to the post office once a week for years.

"Can I help?" the woman asked. She gave a smile but corrected herself, as if she'd been instructed not to.

"Hi," Liza said. For a moment she thought she would tell the woman that she'd been kidnapped, that she needed to call her father. "I hope you can help me."

The woman's earrings were of pink kittens playing with yarn.

"I like those," Liza said, pointing to the earrings.

"What can I do for you?"

"I'm on my way to Wichita Falls," she said. She shook her head once, then looked back at the woman. "To my mother's funeral."

The woman dropped her gaze to her fingers. "I'm sorry to hear that."

"I'm out of gas," Liza said. "If there's anything you could do…" She let the thought stay there a moment.

The woman shook her computer's mouse and looked at her screen like it might hold the answer she was looking for. After a moment, she asked, "Did you check with the Baptist Church down Delaware Street?"

Cody hadn't told her what to say to this question. She was irritated that he'd overlooked this—of course they'd ask if she'd tried to get help elsewhere. Without being entirely sure she'd made the right choice, Liza said, "Yes, ma'am."

"Is there anyone you could call?"

"No."

"Your father?"

"He's dead, too." Liza brushed a piece of hair off her forehead. She was disgusted, impressed at how easy it was for her to say it.

"Well," the woman said, getting out of her chair. "Hold on." Liza thought about walking out, about lying to Cody about the whole thing. She felt certain now that Cody was wrong, that this woman would come back with her hands open and empty, shrugging. She was so surprised when the woman returned with a manila envelope in her hand that Liza started crying.

"It's all right," the woman said. She explained the contents of the envelope. She paused, looked at her fingertips for a moment, then nodded to herself. She fished out a twenty dollar bill from her pocket and stuffed it into Liza's hand.

"It's not much," the woman said, "but it might get you to Wichita Falls."

"You don't have to do that," Liza said.

"God bless you," the woman said.

***

Cody had oozed into Liza's life in increments. First, they exchanged phone numbers about a week after Liza got the job at Fire Tower, just in case either of them needed a shift covered. Then they'd share a joint after work—not every night, just sometimes. He'd text her things like: *Whatcha reading?* or *If you ever want your mind blown, listen to Bach stone sober in the middle of the night. I'll never be the same.* or *Bukowski's brilliance is directly proportionate to his butt-ugliness.* She liked that he insisted on spelling things correctly and writing complete sentences in text messages, something her father refused to do. His texts were desperately misspelled and stubbornly under-punctuated.

One night, after they finished hosing down the floor mats, Cody asked Liza if she wanted to walk him home.

"My car's right here," she said.

"So what?" he replied. "It won't kill you to walk back by yourself."

"All right," she said. "But if I get murdered by methheads I'll haunt you forever."

"I'll take that risk," he said.

As they walked the four blocks together, Liza noticed how empty the streets were, how after ten at night Helena seemed to stop existing, as if when the sun went down everyone froze in place, only to come to at dawn. He told her about his childhood: his father left when he was young, was probably dead; His brother hopped trains, had for about ten years. She told about hers, and for some reason, maybe because she was stoned, she didn't skip over the fact that her mother had disappeared when she was a kid, how her father had been royally nuts about her, how Liza figured he still was, but refused to talk about it.

"Shit," Cody said after she'd finished. They were outside his house, a rickety-looking duplex with paintskins peeling off the window frames and plastic toys scattered around the grass like mines. Even though the windows were dark, Liza kept expecting someone— Cody's wife—to burst through the front door and come after her. "Moms are important. Dads you can do without, but losing a mom can really fuck you up."

After that, things changed quickly, but organically. It didn't feel rushed. At work, she liked the way he touched her back as he walked by to get whole milk from the cooler. She liked the way he smiled at her for no reason at all. She liked how, when they made love for the first time, he didn't apologize for anything, how he just did things without pause and didn't ask if it was good or if he came too quickly or if she came at all. When it was over, he just said, "You thirsty?" and offered her a drink from his water bottle. While he was on top of her in the backseat of her car, the door's window crank pushing into her skull, she couldn't help thinking of what her father might do if he pulled up and saw her with him.

If she couldn't sleep, she'd drive by his house, wondering what it might be like to make love to him in his bed rather than a Target parking lot. She'd even wondered what it might be like to take a vacation with him, to drive to Seattle for the weekend and visit Kurt Cobain's house.

She didn't think it would feel like this.

Liza spotted Cody pacing near the mouth of an alley. His knuckles were red and he kept shaking his hand as if it had fallen asleep.

"How'd you do?" he asked. He walked back and forth across the dirt, stirring up red clouds around his feet.

"There's no 401K anymore, is there?" Liza asked, handing him the envelope.

Cody opened it and pulled out its contents. "Fifteen-dollar gas card and a five-dollar gift card to McDonald's." He crumpled the envelope and dropped it to the ground. "Fuck."

"What now?" she asked. She couldn't bring herself to mention the twenty, felt as if doing so would somehow change their situation irreparably.

Cody pulled out a cigarette from behind his ear, lit it, then handed it to Liza. "That bitch filed for divorce. 401K's locked until we settle in court."

"Sorry," Liza said. She kissed his forehead and pulled him to her chest. He stayed for a moment.

He said, "I called my friend. He might be able to pay us for our services."

"What services?" Liza asked.

A group of children on bicycles pedaled past. One, a deeply tanned boy with a Sooners cap turned backwards, went up for a wheelie, then stuck his tongue out at his friends.

"Jesus," Cody said. "Those boys should be wearin' shoes. They'll rip their toes off."

"Time to go back," Liza said, disappointed, relieved. "The gig's up."

"No, it isn't." He took a penny out of his pocket and flicked it at a sun-battered Chevy Astro parked in front of them. "The money always runs out. We'll always have to do something to get more."

This is the perfect time, she thought. Walk around the corner, call Dad. He'll get you on the next plane. But, as she watched Cody's eyes close, she knew he was running numbers in his head, calculating just how they'd escape this mess. Could they make it to Peru? she wondered. If they did, would things be all right?

She put her arms around his shoulders and kissed him on the chin. "Let's go meet your friend."

Liza's mother simply left one day. No fighting. No note. Though she couldn't remember things during this time so well, she knew that her father seemed to disappear, too. He filed a missing person report. He spent hours in interrogation rooms getting insulted by detectives. He hung posters. He talked to the papers, radio stations, television reporters. He drove to Great Falls, Missoula, Spokane, Billings. He lost the hair on the top of his head. He took more vacation time than he was allowed. He bought boxes of wine and drank in the bathroom with the door locked.

She had only one vivid memory, one she couldn't shake: about a week after her mother disappeared, Liza sat in the living room watching cartoons. It was dark outside, probably cold. She heard a sound—constant and unintelligible, like the hooting of an owl—coming from outside. When she opened the backdoor, she realized that the sound she heard came from her father, clomping around the woods behind their property, calling her mother's name. Six months later, her mother called and said to the answering machine: "I'm sorry, Brian. I don't want to be a wife or a mother anymore. It isn't your fault. I don't need any money."

Later, after she had turned fourteen and her father had remarried, Liza found a shoebox full of artifacts about her mother. Her father had kept a notebook filled with details he heard on the voicemail: a car honking, a train whistle (a foghorn?), someone coughing, the sound of rain on an awning. The box also contained a parking ticket with her mother's name on it from Arizona, a map of California with a town called Willitts circled in blue and yellow highlighter. Her mother's disappearance held him captive, it seemed to Liza, tethered to that moment when he realized his wife hadn't been the victim of something mysterious and terrible, that she wasn't coming back.

As Cody steered them through dusk-struck Oklahoma, red and purple and flat, heading toward another stranger who might take pity on them, Liza couldn't shake the feeling that her running off reminded her father of the way his first wife, the mother of his only child, left. Still, she couldn't will herself to pick up the phone.

"You know the best part about Peru?" Cody asked. They were parked outside of a bar called The Tyrant. Cody passed her a Steel Reserve he bought with change he found under the driver's seat.

"Your friend's late," Liza said. They'd been there for forty-five minutes. Her phone vibrated: a text from her father. *Just tell me where u r then ill leave u b.*

"If you go to the can over there, you'll be in better hands than a free man."

"How's that?"

He lit a cigarette, searched the radio until he found a crackly Earth, Wind & Fire song. "The prison's form of government, run by the inmates, is more efficient than the entire country's.

"They got industry, money, rig-free elections." He offered Liza the smoke, but she refused it. "What's the matter?" he asked.

"Maybe we should turn ourselves over to the cops as soon as we get there."

"They got 1,879 bird species in Peru," he said. "We should become experts, give tours to Americans."

"I'm sure there're plenty of tours already."

"How many in perfect, American English?"

"Let's stick with prison—that plan's fucking brilliant." She'd meant it as a joke, or at least she'd wanted Cody to think it was a joke, but she could feel his eyes on her, could sense his face tightening up, his jawbone bouncing up and down. She'd seen him this way before, when he'd talk about his wife.

"What's daddy sayin'?" Cody asked, pointing to Liza's phone. The last bit of sunset burned out; finally night had arrived.

"He called the F.B.I.," Liza said. "They're gonna swoop down on us any second."

Cody let out a bark-like laugh. "They won't take us alive."

He snatched the phone from her hands and read through her father's texts.

"God," he said. "He's obsessed with you."

"Fuck you."

A black Dodge truck pulled up next to them. Its back window was patched with clear plastic. A tall bald man got out and leaned down so his face was level with Liza's window.

"Cody," the man said.

Cody got out of the car and the two men hugged. They spoke

quietly for a minute, whispering inside jokes and laughing too hard at them.

Cody turned back to her. "French, I'd like you to meet my Liza."

In the glow of the dome light, she could see a small piece of skin like the lifted corner of a strip of scotch tape sticking up from the top of French's head. His beard was graying like her father's. He stuck his hand into the car.

"Pleasure," he said.

"How do you know this one?" Liza asked, pointed toward Cody.

French looked over his shoulder and considered this a moment. "We worked together, years ago."

"Where?" she asked. "He's had so many jobs, it's hard to keep track."

French leaned away from the car, put a thumb over his left nostril, and then blew as hard as he could through his right.

Cody clapped his hands. "What'd you got for us tonight, hombre?"

French stood up. "Have a drink with me," he said, motioning toward the bar. "I wanna run somethin' past you." Without waiting for an answer, he started walking toward the bar. "Nice to meet you," he called over his shoulder.

"Asshole," Liza said.

"Who?" Cody asked, grinning. "Me?"

"Let's get out of here."

"It'll just take a second."

"I don't like him."

Cody leaned through the driver's side window, puckered his lips and let them hang there, waiting for her. "Lay one on me."

"He's waiting for you," she said. She didn't turn toward him until she heard his footsteps crinkling across the parking lot.

Her father texted again. *I dont understand. R u injured? R u on drugs? Do u have enough money?*

Liza looked around the console for a cigarette, but there weren't any.

She typed *I'm fine, Dad*, but couldn't press send. It looked cold, cruel, shining brightly at her in the darkness. For years she'd been angry at her mother for leaving them, mainly for doing such a terrible thing to Dad. She'd missed her, of course, usually when she saw other girls with their mothers—getting dropped off at the mall, or scolded at a stoplight, mother's finger wagging, daughter's eyes pointed at the dashboard. But this sadness was fleeting, more superficial, she knew, than the anger beneath. For years, she'd imagined running into her mother again. Liza would be on a horse in the desert, and she'd come upon her mother, propped up by a cactus, dying of thirst. Or she'd be in New York City in a white limousine and spot her mother digging in a trash bin. Or she'd be in some rusty part of Los Angeles and see her mother, clad in fishnets and a plastic-looking miniskirt, being dragged by a man with jug-handle ears into an abandoned warehouse. She always responded the same way: she left her mother to rot.

A couple, arms locked, walked out of the dark and into the halo of a streetlight. The woman held her head down and had a hand covering her mouth—either laughing or crying, Liza figured. She wondered where her mother might be right now, what she might be doing. New Orleans, working as a dental hygienist? Pittsburgh, selling peanuts at a football stadium? Was she still alive, or did she suffer a stroke or lose a long-fought battle against ovarian cancer or AIDS or typhoid? Did she have new people in her life, a new family? Did her mother wake up some nights and wonder what Liza was up to, what grades she was getting, if she was involved in sports or speech and debate club, whether or not she made her lovers wear condoms? What did her father do to make her mother vanish like that?

Cody and French walked out of the bar smiling, spraying pea gravel with every step.

"French is gonna help us out a little bit," Cody said, getting into the car.

"How nice of him."

He lit a cigarette, handed it to her, then dipped into his pocket and pulled out a clamshell of bills. He fanned them through his fingers, put them to her nose; they smelled like sweat and cinnamon gum. "The only thing is," he said, squinting into the dark for a moment. "You're gonna have to do somethin' weird."

"Me?" she asked. "What the hell?" She hadn't realized how scared she was until she heard her voice—unsteady, high-pitched. She hated her voice, hated Cody for putting her in this position, for not telling French to take his money and go suck an egg. "Does he want me to fuck him?"

Cody turned to her now with his mouth open. He clucked his tongue, shook his head. "Give me more credit than that, will ya?"

"I don't want it." She moved her arm to toss the money out the window, a stupid gesture, one she knew she'd never go through with. Cody caught her at the wrist, held her in place. She turned to him, saw his jaw bone jumping like crazy.

"Don't be a bitch," he said. "Act like a fucking adult."

French turned down a well-lit street flanked on both sides by stores Liza recognized—Best Buy, Target, JC Penny. Cody followed. She took out her phone, scrolled through her contacts, let her thumb hang above her father's number.

"All you gotta do is allow yourself to get pantsed in a public place on camera," he said.

She laughed. "Pantsed? Gimme a break."

He smiled, moved his hand to her leg. "That's not what he called it, but that's what it is, practically. It'll be a piece of cake."

"What'd he call it?"

"Sharking."

She shifted to the other side of the seat, causing his hand to fall off of her. She'd never heard the term, but she didn't like the sound of it. It made her think of sharp knives, missing limbs, broken pieces of brick pelting the side of her head. "I'm not doing that." In the parking lots, cars were buttoned in neat rows all the way to the entrance of each store. French slowed down at the gaped-mouth entrance of a Wal-Mart, crawling to ten miles per hour before deciding to drive on at the last moment. "What the hell's he doing?" Liza asked.

"Three hundred dollars, babe."

"And then what?" she asked.

"Then Peru."

"We don't have passports, plane tickets." She stuck a finger in his face. "You don't have any idea what you're doing."

"I'll take care of all that." He took hold of her finger and holstered it in between her legs. "He sells the videos in Iceland or something, so you don't have worry."

"I could Google 'pervert sharks woman' and see if you're right."

"No one would do that here," Cody said. "That's my point. Americans want to see pregnant girls bite off some tied-up schmuck's nipples."

French turned into a Safeway.

"No one you know'll see this," he said. "Trust me."

Liza and Cody sat in silence. French was smoking a cigarette in his truck; Liza focused on the orange tip, how it grew brighter when he brought it up to his mouth and took a drag. Cody kept sighing and clearing his throat, signaling her to turn toward him. She knew that if she did, he'd give her that look—eyebrows up, mouth almost in a smile—the one that said, "I've been down this road before, you should follow my lead," and she'd comply.

"Babe," Cody said, touching her hand.

She moved away from him. She said, "Give me a cigarette."

"We're out." He held up their crumpled pack. "We're out of everything."

A Toyota Tercel pulled into the parking spot next to French's truck. A stocky man wearing a black sweatshirt with the hood pulled up got out and walked to French's window.

"Who's that?" Liza asked.

The man and French kept looking toward Liza. What would they do if I ran, she wondered, or got out of the car and started yelling? The man stepped back so French could get out the cab. He motioned for Cody and Liza to follow.

"Let's go," Cody said.

"I'm not going," she said, but she found herself opening the door anyway. And when Cody met her at the hood of her car, she allowed him to take her hand and lead the way.

French pulled out a box from the bed of his truck, unfolded it, and took out its contents. "Here's what I want you to wear," he said, handing Liza an orange tube-top dress and a blonde wig.

"Where should I change?" she asked. She held the wig away from her. "How many people've worn this thing?"

"Change here," he said. "It's too suspicious to walk in there with clothes in your goddamn hand."

"Jesus," she said. "Right here?"

"You can do it in the car," Cody offered.

"Your hair's too short," French said. "Take off your bra and panties. Remember this: aisle fourteen. Home and Housewares." He held up a finger with one hand and four with the other. "Fourteen. That's where it goes down. I'll be following you with the video camera before that, but don't pay attention to me. You're shopping. Put shit in your cart. Knock on melons. Sniff avocados."

She nodded, but kept her eyes on Cody. He was tearing a wadded paper towel with the toe of his shoe. She was suddenly aware of a sort of high-pitched, rattling sound. She looked around, but couldn't find the source, and it seemed to be getting louder. "What the hell's that sound?"

"Cicadas," Cody said.

"How do you know?" Liza said. "You don't know anything."

"Don't lollygag," French said, "But don't rush, either. Remember: shop."

She took off her shirt; Cody stood in front of her, blocking her from French and the other man.

"She's not an idiot," Cody said. "You don't have to act like she's a goddamn kid."

She turned to him. "Mind your own business," she said. "Go play 'daddy' for someone else."

Out of the corner of her eye, Liza saw French look away. "Go on," she said to French.

"In aisle fourteen, reach for a red spatula," French said. "It'll be towards the center—you'll see it."

The guy in the hooded sweatshirt lit up a cigarette.

"Give me one of those," Liza said. As she bent down to take off her underwear she held onto Cody's shoulder for balance.

She heard her phone vibrate in her shorts pocket: a number she didn't know. *Garrett wants to tell his dad goodnight.* Oh, Liza thought, shit. She handed the phone to Cody. "Your wife."

He looked surprised. He put his hand out to take the phone, then paused. "What's she want?"

Liza pushed it toward him. "Find out for your fucking self."

"Pay attention," French said, snapping his fingers. "I'm almost through."

"Hey," Cody said. "Listen." Liza turned away from him, nodded for French to go on.

"Once your arm's fully extended, Bart's gonna pull the dress to your ankles," French said. He coughed into his elbow. "Gasp, but don't scream—we don't want assholes going concerned-citizen on us. Still, look surprised, cover yourself up quickly." He smiled. "It should be good."

Cody was on the phone now, his back toward Liza. "What?" he asked. "I can't hear you, pal."

"That's all he's gonna do?" Liza asked, pointing her thumb at Bart. Though it was dark, it looked like his fingers were blackened, maybe by oil or tar. She imagined his fingers digging into her flesh as he pulled down the dress—would whatever the hell was on his fingers give her an infection? Cellulitis? Tetanus? Would she be able to get treated for that in Peru? She pictured straw huts with crude, drippy red crosses painted on them, and inside the waiting room chickens pecking around the patients' bare feet. Shut up, she thought. You don't know anything about Peru.

Cody walked in dazed semi-circles, holding one foot out while balancing on the other. "That's great," he said. "I miss you, too, bud." He reached the outer circle of light thrown from one of the parking lot's fixtures; Liza could see that he was smiling, laughing. She couldn't hear him anymore, but that didn't matter.

"Ready?" French asked. He had his camera out now, its little red light glowing thirstily.

Bart, who was smoking his third cigarette by Liza's count, nodded gravely. He put on a black stocking cap and rolled it down; he'd cut eyeholes into it. He straightened it out, so that the eyeholes were perfectly aligned, then rolled it back up on his forehead. All she could see of his face when he put his hood up was the slight, grayish glint of cars' headlights reflecting off his teeth.

"You?" French asked her.

She looked for Cody, but he'd wandered out of sight. She looked across the parking lot to the busy street and watched the blurry red of taillights moving down the road. Above the crackle of cicadas, Liza heard a whistling sound—a train, she thought. She pictured it: large, black, almost invisible in the darkness, a fairytale trail of steam chugging into the sky. She listened to its loud song until she was through the sighing pneumatic doors and into the blinding florescence, where the sounds of registers beeping and cashiers calling over the PA system were the only things Liza could hear.

BLACK & WHITE

Things are not
as they once were, an

empress in the golden
age of cinema. Tongue-

tied and twisted just
an early glow morning

lifted above soil. Terrors
cross-faded at a

signal. It's these
small town politics

that give me the red
ass, he said with

another drip of his
IV and pump of his

compression plates. These
things have a way of

building the history
of television into

them.

ONE MORE LETTER

Another sand
that gets into
         nails
         and

         walls
it shut my
pandering love

to my gills. Oh,

the fish are here
today to bite

any dead skin you
keep neglecting
but then it turned

into a house we can
miss again. I

forgot you were
there too, really.

QUINCUNX

If this is all, quit your hold.
Bury your imprint far
from me. No more writhing,
my slivered sun.

All that touching was witchcraft. Still,

at the crux I remember sharply
god's hand at every turn
and the saltiness of donning you
in a room without law.

Two fires that cannot yoke.
How damn starry it is

every time you strobe near—

LEORA FRIDMAN

WHAT I WANT FROM A COUNTRY

Call me yellow
for World War II.

Call me a
flaming pinko.

I will always
find the color

I need.
We live

in a day
where I

do not fight.
This is not

my womanhood
or my lesson:

I can visit
tonight

if I must.
How much

do you need me
in cost.

A plane ticket.
A victory garden.

Car parts melted
in war planes.

VEDRAN HUSIĆ

THE POET FROM MOSTAR

The checkpoint is on Rude Hrozničeka, between the building I grew up in and the one I occupy now as a soldier. Behind my former building the land runs down to the Neretva River, green, transparent water sloshing against blue and grey rocks. The Serbs destroyed the nearest bridge a year ago; a small dam formed from the debris where the river curves narrowly. I walk around my old neighborhood in a soldier's uniform, jungle-colored, tight around the shoulders, and boots in whose black I can never see my reflection. Our headquarters are in a couple of third floor apartments (#9 and #10) whose prior occupants left when war broke out a second time. There are birds on the useless telephone wires and children below in the yard of my former building. The gap echoes and glares. The birds are sparrows. The barefoot girls, in the shade of a skinny linden, clap their hands and sing an old rhyme, while the perspiring boys, heads bowed, rummage in the overgrown grass, their pockets bulging with bullet shells. People in the neighborhood recall when a Jeep full of drunk Serb paramilitary drove over the bridge that wasn't there, the nothingness that stretches from one side to the other, and crashed into the rocks and debris. At night all one can see is the moving darkness of the water.

All we shoot are birds, Mario says. He says it all the time. He falls on his knees in front of the open window, grabs his rifle and puts it into position. He closes his left eye and, slitting the right, lets his finger slide up and down the curve of the trigger. Even when I can't see them, I hear the cling clang of the shells in their pockets and know where they are. Leaning out of windows, their mothers constantly check on them, shouting instructions in bright, exhausted voices. Mario was one of the young men who dived every summer from the crowded Old Bridge into the cold water below. Sometimes he shouts threats down on the street at Prof. Abdić, who walks from his building to the checkpoint and back in a dirty shirt and sweatpants, his hands clasped behind him, one shoulder held higher than the other. Imbedded in my mind with the bridge itself is the straight, stoic form of those bodies, startlingly balanced in mid-air, plunging into the green transparency of the river and producing a sharp, ripping sound on entry. You're in the crosshairs, Emir, Mario yells from the pedestal of our third floor window, and Prof. Abdić waves meekly at the jokes of his former student, his other hand shielding his eyes from the sun. Death is instant, and what's left of the sparrow is only a kaleidoscopic puff of feathers.

This is Mostar, a place the children in the yard have heard called home by the same mouths that unashamedly call it hell. Prof. Abdić walks the allowed length of street he grew up and lived his entire life on, reciting poetry to himself like a madman. Before the war, he was a professor of Russian Literature at the University of Mostar, one of the four professors who for years gathered each Friday in our living room to play cards. I remember a room filled with blue cigarette smoke and the bitter whiff of plum brandy; the strange harmony that existed between the voices and the night, the former growing louder as the latter grew darker; I remember the rolled up sleeves and undone top buttons, the black chips shining in the center of the table. I watch them play, unfolding my chair in front of my old building and acquiring a full view of the oval yard, consisting of a grass-less patch of pebbles in the center where the children congregate shoulder to shoulder before a game of dodgeball, facing Sanel, who holds a blue rubber ball in his hands. Sanel is the oldest—he is thirteen—and tallest of them all, dark-haired and in denim overalls. Tina, the captain of the opposing team, is long-legged, pony-tailed and sleepy-eyed. I remember my own childhood and the games we played, and I think to myself that growing up during war is the most unnatural thing in the world.

The front is three kilometers from our checkpoint; we get almost no direct fire and there is nothing to do. The smell across the river is ash; the sound, man-made thunder. When the war came to Mostar in the spring of '92, my family and I escaped to Croatia, an uneventful journey, half of it spent with my head between my knees. The Serbian siege of Mostar ended in June and we returned home in early August. But there was no home. There was the caved-in roof, the blackened apartments, the crumbling staircase, and the wonder of why the Serbs chose to bomb our building, but leave untouched the one connected to it. It was to Rodoč then, to my grandparents' house, where we lived out the uneasy peace. Cafés reopened amongst the rubble and, dutifully, people came to drink. A halfhearted reconstruction of the city began. From time to time, the Serbs lobbed a bomb from the mountains to remind us of their close proximity. Then, in May of '93, the new war started (within the still-ongoing war north and east of us) between the Bosnian Catholics and Bosnian Muslims, ending the increasingly sinister peace in Mostar.

Mr. Abdić writes poems in his empty apartment; sometimes during his evening walks, he reads them aloud to me, his most perceptive student in peacetime, his only student now. Some are about the sparrows on the useless telephone wires; others are about the boys hunting for bullet shells, their pockets singing. By the end of the first week of the new war, most of the male Muslim population on the west side was either deported to the east, with their families, or detained, alone, in Heliodrom, the prison camp in Rodoč that was previously a military airport. In rare cases, like a visit from the Red Cross, men are allowed to temporarily leave the camp and go home. Such a privilege was given to Prof. Abdić, because of his chronic back pain and connections within the camp. His wife and two daughters are in Germany. They fled before the Serb invasion; he came back alone during the short peace – which lasted just long enough to get his hopes up, he says – and was arrested when the new war started. Most of his poems are about the past: two lovers illuminated by the milky glow of a lamp on Lučki Bridge; an impromptu family picnic on the pebbled bank of the Neretva; an aproned baker on Fejić passing loaf after loaf to a blue-uniformed delivery man. I tell him I hear in his poems the moan of a sidewalk accordion and the ragged chorus of voices in Old Town cafes. I don't ask him why he returned because it's a stupid question and he expects better of his best student.

In the bedroom of #10 the windows are always open. Bottles of beer and homemade plum brandy, cans of soda and old newspapers are scattered all over the room. The wind sweeps up crumbs of food and sends them across the parquet, but it can't clear out the damp, acidic smell of sweat that hangs in the air. Graffiti covers one side of the wall, the others punctured with bullet holes. Occasionally, a cockroach crawls up and down the floor. It's the regret with which Mario says it that irritates me. He is on his knees, his left eye closed. Led Zeppelin's "Whole Lot of Love" jerks out of the radio he has brought from home, blending with the howl and wail of the children outside, drowning out the distant gunfire. I have never fired a shot, except in the air. His finger stops moving; a cigarette, unlit, dangles from the corner of his mouth. Sometimes I want to pummel him with all my strength, beat him into an awareness of suffering beyond his own. But then I think of what will happen if he fights back. Or worse, if he doesn't? The mess and the music gives the place a dorm room atmosphere, and I often imagine we are students freely indulging in this lifestyle rather than soldiers confined to it by war. We are twenty.

Don't shoot, Mario, I say. There are children out there. Prof. Abdić says that the nature of memory and time is like the nature of darkness and water and I don't quite know what he means. I met Mario in Rodoč, where I spent my weekends as a child and where he was born, and where our games consisted of chasing frenzied chickens and tormenting a chained goat. Once school started, we progressed to more ordinary games like dodgeball and soccer. Mario takes out the Makarov pistol he bought in Bulgaria before the war; he points it at the side of his head. He is in his undershirt, cargos and boots, forgetful of past and present. The sweat shows underneath his armpits. The sky is dark and enormous, and after the laughter hushes and the clinking of bottles stops, the only sound comes from the mad concord of the crickets around us. Children move invisible in the night, real and imagined, their eyes bright and feral in the dark. Prof. Abdić carries photographs on him at all times, inside the waistband of his sweatpants: one of himself and his wife, snowflakes melting on their black coats, one each of his two daughters, and one of a crowd of Velež fans running onto the field to celebrate the Cup win in 1983 (a man has both feet off the ground at the moment the snapshot is taken, seeming to levitate). The past, Prof. Abdić likes to say, is a world of echoes and half-forgotten songs.

I remember a blue-eyed boy with long blond locks, a boy who got carrot-red freckles in the summer, a boy who, following the very first day of school, ran after the teacher, pulling on his jacket, to ask him if we needed to come back tomorrow. In one of his poems Prof. Abdić compares the destruction of the Old Bridge to an angered child tearing up the Mother's Day card he had so carefully crafted because he desired, in his malicious rashness, to inflict the most immediate pain. But that's just metaphor. Prof. Abdić's eyes are spinach-green and he's as short as Pushkin. In sweet grimy adolescence, when I began to write poetry, Mario took up the guitar, each envious of the other's limited talent. For hours everyday he strummed on that acoustic guitar of his, while I intermittently sang. Or we'd both be singing along to Western songs on the radio. In the evenings, we went out, always together, watching movies in the overcrowded cinema in the city with friends whose ethnicity and religion seemed completely unimportant. It will all come back to us one day, Prof. Abdić says, and then we will stand in front of each other cleansed and ashamed. His poem ends when Ottoman sultan Suleiman the Magnificent, whose image I remember from a painting in which he is depicted in profile, wearing a black shawl and an outsized white turban, commissions the building of the bridge.

Mario, mumbling to himself, lays the Makarov on the ground and leans back in the folding chair. He complains loudly of a headache because he is drunk. The light of the lamppost shines off his shaved head, and I feel betrayed by the sight of it. He smiles a wicked smile but its wickedness is halfhearted. Do you hear me? I say. Don't shoot. He is silent. Are you listening? I come closer. Under the strain of their shared fatherlessness, Prof. Abdić intones, gesturing with one hand, the other holding the paper, though he does not read off it. Shaved and gaunt, he looks older than he is, with dark-colored pouches under his green eyes. The perspiring boys hop from hot concrete onto cool grass, hunting for bullet shells. But in an instance their task is forgotten, when the white tank slinks closer, slowly, like an armored cloud. We give the UNPROFOR soldiers a hard time at the checkpoint. Smurfs, we call them, though we know they can destroy us instantly. But they won't. Blue and white are colors entirely too cheery for war, boys, Mario yells as they pass in their wheeled tanks. We are as much observers as they are, but this is our country and we don't pretend to be able to will the war out of existence.

"How useless this is. Being a soldier, I mean."

"Because there's nothing to do?"

"Because it's just useless. Bombing our own city. You can't cross the Neretva, can't go to the other side. But that's Old Town. That's where all the good restaurants are."

"Would you prefer if the entire city was bombed?"

"Yes. I mean no. No because I live here. I don't know. All I know, all I have ever known with any certainty, is that I don't want to kill or to die."

"So that's your point. You're a coward."

This conversation only happens in my head and even there I can't make him understand. It's a lack of imagination, Prof. Abdić would say.

Prof. Abdić says he began writing poetry at fifteen, when it became impossible not to. His early poems were terrible, contrived and quickly abandoned, barely worth the cheek of the girls they were dedicated to. There were many, he says. As a student at the University of Mostar, where he would later teach, he started writing political poems and imagined stopping tanks with his pen, sparking peaceful revolutions, imagined his poetry being recited in crowded city squares by zealous youths, hungry and betrayed. But there was no spark and no fire, no knock on the door by the authorities, no condemnation or medal. My country didn't need my poetry, he says, or my silence. Mario picks the Makarov back up from the ground and points it at Robert, who has a screwdriver in his hand. The drunken cheering begins again and Robert dares him to do it. Mario's eyes are red; he says the gun is not loaded; he leans back in the chair, his stomach lowering and rising as if from great exertion. Someone has set a tire aflame; the orange and white-paneled barricades gleam in the bonfire. Sweat runs down Robert's neck and he groans under a sky enormous and dark, charged with our madness and fire. There is a military van in the yard, a yellow Jugo missing a tire. Once the laugher dies down, there is only the sound of the blinking crickets. Through the thin envelope I can read the last lines of Prof. Abdić's letter to his wife, which I send for him: I'm as unthinking and unfeeling as a stone. I have only enough for these letters. Breaking up parts of what I have written here into stanzas might yield a poem. Not a good one, but a familiar one, and maybe of some comfort to you. Love, Emir.

Out of the bedroom of #10, "Gimmie Shelter" can be heard, above us the chirping of sparrows, and behind us the pop of an occasional explosion. On a manhole in the yard of my old building, bullet shells, lined up in ascending order, glint in the sunlight. Tina walks an alley looking for her vanilla pudding among the leftover candies the UNPROFER soldiers have distributed. She stops suddenly, only to rub her foot against her calve. Prof. Abdić and I walk up and down the street we grew up on, talking of literature, and the soldiers working on the lights of one of the barricades call "Muslim lover" and "dead man walking" after us. I have taught my daughters, Prof. Abdić says, to be blind to religious differences, to consider themselves the only ideal ethnicity, a Yugoslav, and to follow the ethics, the rainbow-bright ethics, of humanism. Should I regret now doing what's right? And how can you, the son of a Catholic man who never practiced and a Muslim woman who didn't either but couldn't just forget where she came from, how, forced to wear the uniform of the Croatian Defense Council, how can *you* display with any genuine inner passion the outer appearance of a Catholic and a Croat, or show any real desire for the destruction of a city you love and a people you never hated. When he speaks like that I wonder if the only difference between my view of the war and Mario's is a Muslim mother. If my anger is only disappointment? If you can right someone who you have already forgiven? Tina is offered other candies but refuses. She sits down cross-legged in the pebbled clearing of the yard and throws her arm across her shoulder to scratch her back. We walk up and down the street, talking of *War and Peace, Crime and Punishment, Dead Souls.*

I come closer. "Mario, don't shoot" I say, and kick the rifle off target with my foot, tipping him over like a tower.

"What's the matter with you? I wasn't going to shoot," he says, ascending slowly, in stages, like an illustration of evolving man we saw in books from school.

"I bet you weren't going to shoot."

"If I said I won't then I won't, and if I want to shoot then I will."

"Why are you being an idiot?"

"They're just fucking birds."

"What did they ever do to you?"

From my folding chair I watch the children in the center of the yard, one half standing behind Tina, the other half behind Sanel, who flips a coin in the air, catches it in his right hand, brings it down on his left, and rejoices after slowly revealing which side it is, number or flame on the old Yugoslav dinar (slowly, as if extra time would have transformed it if it wasn't in his favor). Then I hear Tina shout and she begins running down the street. The children spring magically to attention and follow after her. Turning into a side street, the tank stops and is surrounded. They bang on the armor, producing a dull, tinkling sound, until a helmeted head pops out of the hatch. The young man, a boy really, looks at the crowd assembled before him and starts throwing candy with a strangely flamboyant flair, like he's on top of a float in a parade. The little beggars push and shove each other, frantically un-tucking their shirts to use them as pouches. Only Tina refuses to push and shove as she searches for her vanilla pudding. After dispensing with all the sweets, the boy disappears into his hole and the tank goes the way it came. Under a green and brown thicket of trees at the edge of the yard, the children gather to eat.

In the folding chair, Mario stretches his arms above his head as if to touch the sky. A child's idea of endlessness. The humidity is unbearable, a heavy wet weight. Or maybe it's the fire, still burning, throwing shadows on the wall of our building, shadow flames dancing in a tribal circle. The Makarov is in his hand again but nobody is paying attention anymore. He smiles at me, a sad lost smile. I'm silent. He points the gun at the side of his head again, slides his finger up and down the smooth curve. I close my eyes. Glass shatters brightly as somebody drops or throws a bottle against the concrete. Mario laughs. The crickets buzz like fire. Time is a river in the dark, Prof. Abdić once said, and we remember against its current. Before my eyes I see twenty pairs of legs run after one ball and kick at it blindly, hitting bone more often than rubber, while faraway adult voices hopelessly instruct us to spread out. I feel the warmth at my back. The sound reaches me before it's made. My eyes are closed. On the other end of the yard, opposite where I sit in my folding chair, the children silently and busily eat, chimerical in the tall grass. Tina gives up her search and walks over to where the others are. One by one she inspects their loot, finding nothing. She turns her bare feet toward her building as the crack of a rifle rings out. Then the sound of the bullet striking brick. Then silence. Huddled together in the high grass, the children wait for a sign to move. A few women stray out into the yard. Tina wipes the palms of her hands on her shorts. Overhead, the sparrows reassemble on the useless telephone wires.

When the time comes, it is up to me to chaperon Prof. Abdić back to the camp. I wait outside of his building for Mario to arrive with the car. When he does, we go upstairs together to the third floor, and Mario raps on the professor's door with the butt of his rifle. You are a selfish idiot, I tell him. He looks at me stupidly and hurt. The door opens and the professor greets us kindly, in dirty shirt and sweatpants, dropping his bagful of belongings on the floor and getting down on one knee to tie his worn sneakers, only the right, for the left has no laces. Halfway down the last dusty flight of stairs, he suddenly stops. "I have to go to the bathroom," he says, his eyes fixed on the curved end of the banister.

"No, absolutely not," Mario says, pulling open the building door a touch, the light squeezing in like a cat. "Just hold it."

"Please, I must go."

"You should have gone before."

"But I must go now."

"Just let the man go to the bathroom," I say. Mario slams the door shut and leans against it. He lights a cigarette. "Let's go," I say to the professor. "Thank you," he says in the doorway of his apartment, putting his bag down. His smile is childish, his green eyes moist and deep. I look away. "Give my regards to your father," he says, and goes into the bathroom. Hearing the click of the lock, I go down the hallway that has a door on either side and leads into the living room. Filled with light because there are no curtains, the living room is empty of furniture except for a couch and a makeshift table. The soft innards of the couch jut out through a rip in one of the red cushions, and the table is a shaded window glass laid on the flat seat of a back-less chair. On this table, along with a thick lilac-gray coating of dust, is a copy of Dostoevsky's *The Possessed*. I sit down on the couch and begin to read. I read for a while before I hear the hard, flat pounding of boots on the stairs outside the apartment, which I then can't un-hear. I re-read the same sentence, word by word, but it reveals no meaning I can understand. The front door opens with a splinter and a thud. I throw the book on the table and run to the bathroom; in the hallway, I tell Mario to shut up and get away from the bathroom door. I put my ear to the wood. No sound. Prof. Abdić, are you ready? I say. No answer. I knock once, then knock again; I beat on the door with my palm; Emir, I yell. I turn the knob with force and the door gives easily. He lies on his stomach, heaped on the floor, a black puddle spreading from under his throat like velvet, like ink. The blade half of a straight razor glints coldly on the tiles. Mario drags his body out from between the toilet and tub and puts one hand over the other and pushes against his chest. His movements are slow and vague, as if performed underwater. He yells at me, tells me to do something. I just stand there. His hands sink slowly in and rise slowly out. On the wall, reaching the ceiling, a dark splatter of blood, warm as cooked jam.

I walk around my old neighborhood, hunching my shoulders against the wind. My boots hurt my toes as I walk. I turn toward Prof. Abdić's former building and run into the boys by the rosebush-flanked entrance, forming a circle around something on the ground; I yell and they scatter. Ringed by rocks that they must have gathered, the carrion of a small bird lies prone on the grass. One wing is spread out and the other half-covers its gray belly and dark throat. Its bronze head is turned to one side, the lead-blue beak slightly open. The bird is a sparrow. Ants are moving over its corpse, wrapping it in a quivering black blanket. I stare down at the diminishing sparrow. I feel the sun on my neck. The wind makes me shiver, but I keep staring. And if one of the boys happens now to come back, he will see me bent over and shivering in the sun, frozen like in a picture, and he will think I am shedding tears over a dead bird.

APPEAL

Say, *ripple*. Hold it in your mouth.
That is what I am when I think of you.

I wrote, *The slugs here are orange.*
But I meant: *longing—*

everything is out of its shell, littering the grass.

The lake shuffles as a card deck.
I can't single out a card; I can't single out a wave.

Or what it means to hold you in my mouth.

BRAD VOGLER

12.28/29.12/4.20.13

cog
wick
work(s) sings

a holden to o –
                over air &

wet step(s) in graveled muck

field heart
amputated

I could return to look

12.30.12/1.2/3.13

warbled seeing/sight : landscape

yearning : thistle of pinches

to populate a house such :
table : chair

     you
     a second chair

these are the small holds allowed to sentence

SAM THAYN

HALF-LOVER

I.

Make me good again, you say, and I leave my hands home next time so I can try. We never get tangled up the same way twice. I'm flexible, you assure me, and your toes are always *en pointe*. I used to crave ballerinas, but only the kind in air. When they land I am regretful. There's a play opening in your ears and I am in the front row asking where the bathroom is.

II.

If I see you again, it will be at the bottom of the statue in your image, the arms broken away and the head carried off and the perfect breasts. Your legs will be stained with centuries. I will take you home and wrap you in your winter coat until your torso thaws. And you will love me. And we will find your head in the arms of your sleeping daughter.

III.

Passing over my mouth like a stream, the red taste of memory. I smile at your long broken neck. I smile at your fenced-off doll parties. Every backyard has a pool and every pool has the foot of a king in it. Your father is outside grilling and the clouds dot his eyes. He'll make a fine addition to the city cemetery.

IV.

When I drive to the city, you are a skyscraper. The clouds at your
throat. I put my hand over your face and that's when you see me:
the only train in the desert. The blinking red lights on the face of
the dog buried in our backyard.

V.

A box of eels sent overnight at your door. Sign here, we said,
crowding your stoop. Sign here and here and here. Your son became an angel that night. And his ribs were showing. We chased
him to the sea and cast his footprints in bronze.

CODY ERNST

CAPSULE

Moneymen paid Julie big bucks
to paint explosions in their lobby,

ones that faced out towards the cardboard
and tear gas crowd. She made

cartographic bird confetti. She gave
her mural flight plans, phosphor holes, and

swamps yapping next to straight-faced
ghosts of biology diagrams.

Powerful Julie worked in this armpit,
fingertipping rockets

into surrounding corn rows. Epicenters
met. Shaven flakes whirled. Julie lived

on this map in an invisible capsule
with comets and streamers digging

her a podium. There were flight
delays. There were comings and leafings.

There were prices, lasers, rises, drops,
and in the end it was like listen,

may death be alright
and reincarnation an upgrade.

FLYING CAT

Here I am, spending another Saturday morning sitting in a beige plastic chair in the packed reception area at the Peace Avenue Veterinary Clinic in Mongkok, shriveling from the cold under the gale force air con, kicking myself for not remembering to wear anything warmer than a T-shirt, waiting for my number to be called. I'm J10 and the electronic light board behind the counter tells me my vet is busy with patient J8. J8 is a portly golden Labrador that can't walk. Two slight looking women lugged him into the surgery inside a large blanket they had doubled over and fashioned into a hammock. It strikes me that this might be J8's last visit. He can't walk and he peed through his blanket as soon as the automatic doors opened and he realized where he was going. I feel sad for J8 and the two women. I stare at the floor, thinking about his last moments when a door opens and the two women reappear, the dog lying down inside his hammock, eyes wide open, very much alive. They fix up the bill, pick up their corners of the sodden blanket and lug J8 out into a waiting car.

I am here with my cat. You can't see him because he is locked inside his polyester blue cat carrier, but he looks like he's just come off the set of *Jurassic Park*. Wire and concrete sprout from his face and two posts on either side of his mouth hold his jaw open. He wears an Elizabethan collar to stop him tugging out the blue plastic feeding tube that pokes through a hole in his neck and keeps him alive.

It's our sixth visit in three weeks. The girls that work here know us now. It helps that I am the only *gweipo* that seems to visit the surgery, but it's the cat too. "Ahh", they say, when I check in at the reception desk, "Flying cat." That's the name they give to cats that fall out of buildings. And my cat has earned his title. In six and a half years of life he has fallen twice.

My vet thinks Hong Kong has the biggest population of flying cats of anywhere in the world. He is probably right. After Macau, Hong Kong is the most densely populated developed urban area on earth. Almost everyone lives in apartments here, and lots of people own cats. Mongkok is one of the most congested parts of Hong Kong, heaving with 130,000 people per square kilometer. In a good week, this surgery, which opens 24 hours and is considered one of the best in Hong Kong, sees an average of one flying cat each day. In a bad week, which tends to happen more in spring and summer when people leave their windows and balcony doors open, they see more than double that. There are seventy vet clinics in Hong Kong. If each clinic sees one flying cat a week, that's 3,640 flying cats in a year, seventy in a week. And that doesn't include the cats that walk away unharmed after their falls or the ones that don't get taken to a vet.

I am a dog person. I *liked* cats, in the way I liked komodo dragons and sharks and all animals except maybe rats, particularly the ones on Hong Kong Island that grow to be the size of terriers, but I had never loved a cat until recently. I owned a cat as a child and it was not an altogether happy experience. Lucy was a gift from my parents for my 11th birthday. She was eight weeks old and looked adorable and none of us had any reason to think she might have a few kangaroos loose in the top paddock. I stopped picking her up a couple of weeks after I got her. I grew tired of being scratched and bitten. My arms looked like they belonged to a disturbed child, the kind who kept botching the job of slicing through her veins.

When she wasn't harming me, Lucy liked to hunt. A bird would do, but her prized catch was the funnel web spider, one of the five deadliest spiders in the world and Australia's most deadly. Funnel webs happened to live on the north shore of Sydney, where we lived. Lucy's favorite trick was to catch a funnel web, hold it gently between her teeth, march up the back steps of our porch, through the cat door, saunter down the hallway to my bedroom, hop onto my bed, and deposit her catch on my pillow. This happened at least a dozen times during my childhood. I know now that cats only share their prey with those they are closest to, and that this was Lucy's way of showing me affection. But I didn't know that then. What I knew was that cats have immunity to funnel web spiders. People do not. At the time I remember thinking Lucy knew that. Scientists didn't discover the anti-venom until 1981, by which time Lucy had realized her real love was birds.

I planned to live the rest of my life cat-free until I moved to

Singapore and fell in love with someone who owned a cat. Gabriella had been given Filippo as a birthday present by her last girlfriend in Milan. After their breakup, Gabriella and Filippo moved to Singapore. They made a strange pair: Gabriella, with a symmetrical face, huge brown eyes and blonde wavy hair, and Filippo, an exotic short-haired Persian, with a thick coat of two tone ginger stripes, and a face that looked like he'd been propelled into a wall at rocket speed.

I suspected Gabriella was the love of my life, but I wasn't sure. She was younger than me and ridiculously good looking and defiant and feisty and everything else I wanted and part of me thought she was a bit too good to be true. Filippo, I decided, was not too good to be true. So I invited him to move in first. Gabriella was spending pretty much every night of the week at my place anyway, and I felt sorry for Filippo, left alone in an empty apartment all day and all night. So Filippo moved in, and aside from an allergy to cats I never knew I had, which required an intensive dose of antihistamines for the next four years, we got on marvelously. I came to love Filippo, and he loved me back. More, it turned out, than he loved Gabriella. Six months later, on the day Gabriella moved in with us, he left a giant poo inside our bathtub, signaling his disgruntlement with the new living arrangements.

Gabriella had plans for another cat, although she didn't make this known until we had lived together for eight weeks. I wanted a dog. Filippo slept 23 hours a day and when he wasn't sleeping he was eating, preening himself, being kissed and cuddled, or using his kitty litter box. He slept between our pillows at night and didn't stir from the moment we fell asleep to the moment we woke. His sleep was frighteningly deep, so much so that I woke from time to time throughout the night and checked for the vein inside his neck, just to make sure he still had a pulse.

One night over dinner, Gabriella suggested that Filippo might enjoy the company of another cat. When, I wondered? His one hour of activity each day seemed pretty much full, and I didn't see him staying awake to squeeze in playtime with a friend. But he was an easy cat, and if we could find another cat like him, two would be no trouble. I had only one condition: cat number two *must* come from the SPCA. I was not prepared to perpetuate the atrocious trade in live animals by buying one from a pet store. Singapore has lax regulations around the sale of animals, and it was known to those of us that cared that pets that didn't get sold by pet stores while they were still young and cute ended up being dumped or killed. I worried about those pets and the stain on my karma.

Gabriella had different ideas. She had found another exotic short-haired Persian cat for sale in a pet store in Holland Village. He was white with amber eyes and a squashed face and looked like something out of a Stephen King novel. "We cannot get this kitten", I said, the first time she picked him up and handed him over to me for a cuddle. "He's sick!" I said, handing him straight back. "Cat flu! Look at the muck around his eyes and nose. He'll make Filippo sick. Maybe even kill him!" But no amount of reason would change her mind, and in the end I got the feeling it might come down to a choice between this kitten and me. And there was no way I was going to win that contest. "Look how miserable he is! If we don't take him they'll kill him!" she said. And I, in love with her and feeling very sorry for this sickly looking cat, relented.

Filippo resented the intrusion, but we had bigger problems. Giorgio, who cost $1000 at the pet store, clocked up a vet bill worth nearly $25,000 in his first three months of life. The pet store gave him cat flu and he came close to dying from it twice. We had finally come to terms with the reality we might lose our kitten, when a friend of a friend recommended a vet who mingled western medicine with homeopathic remedies. Remarkably, Giorgio was cured.

His convalescence over with, Giorgio's personality blossomed. He developed some weird habits, like sitting on his rear two legs with his front legs up like a meerkat, staring at us as we ate dinner, head cocked (the "with curiosity" is all implied.) Tired, he stretched himself along the side of a wall and stuck his legs up in the air and fell asleep. He bolted from the living room to our bedroom and back again in large loops, leaping over us sitting on the sofa or eating at the dining room table. When we got home from work he followed us into the bathroom, waited until we got into the shower, and stole our underpants. He carried them in his mouth through our apartment out to the balcony where the washing machine was and dumped them there. If the TV was on, he would sit on the table beside the screen and tap at the pictures with his paw. His favorite was the National Geographic channel. If a wildlife documentary was showing he would offer his own voice-over in his high-pitched kitten squawk. Unlike Filippo he was nocturnal, and he twigged fast that I was the light sleeper in the family. As soon as I fell asleep he would march up my sleeping body, rub my face with his whiskers, or if he really wanted my attention, lift his tail and grind his moist anus into my mouth.

I had a skateboard I liked to ride up and down the marble hallway of our apartment. Giorgio watched me, and one day after I had done my laps he hopped onto the board, used his front legs to steady himself and his two back legs to push off. He rode the skateboard the whole length of the hallway. It wasn't long before he was turning corners and zipping down the hallway faster than I could. His skill with the skateboard was astonishing and fuelled our belief that Giorgio was a very clever cat. Around this time we stopped watching TV. What could be more entertaining than our own precious cat, given a death sentence by a vet a mere three months earlier, doing tricks on a skateboard? Like any proud parents we were convinced Giorgio was special -a genius probably- and that we would soon retire and live off the proceeds of his extraordinary talents. "See?" Gabriella said as we watched him doing donuts in our living room. "And you didn't want him!"

We were in Manila visiting a friend the first time Giorgio fell. Our plane had just touched down at Ninoy International Airport and we were fighting our way through the scrum of the baggage carousel when Gabriella turned on her phone. There were seven messages from her sister who was cat sitting at our place, each more frantic than the last. Giorgio had vanished. Every cupboard, bookshelf, curtain and crevice had been searched.

He was not inside the apartment.

We rang our friend, apologized for the sudden change of plans, explained that we had no choice but to return to Singapore to find our lost kitten, grabbed our bags, ran up the escalator to the ticketing office, and bought two tickets for the next flight home.

By the time our taxi drove up Scott's Road into Orchard, Giorgio had been found. He had hopped up onto the washing machine in the small open alcove outside our kitchen and fallen four floors. Luckily, he had landed inside the balcony of an apartment on the first floor. He was fine. We took turns checking his legs, his paws, his spine, his teeth, the inside of his ears. There was not so much as a scratch on him. We had barely been home an hour when he climbed back on the skateboard and started doing a circuit of our apartment. Our cat was invincible. It was a miracle. He was one in a million. "See?" Gabriella said. "And you didn't want him!"

Six years passed between Giorgio's two falls. Lots happened in that time. Gabriella and I moved to Hong Kong, lived here four years, nursed Filippo through kidney failure, and split up. But before that, in happier times, our family grew significantly, and we were now the joint owners of three dogs and three cats. In a desperate attempt to make good for the sin of buying Giorgio from a pet store, we adopted our dogs from *Hong Kong Dog Rescue* and our cats from *Hong Kong Alley Cat Watch*. Each new addition fitted into our family seamlessly, and our three stray dogs loved their feline siblings. Our break up was sad, for me at least, but we wanted it to be amicable and agreed that our kids had to come first. We found apartments in adjoining blocks on the Kowloon side of Hong Kong and agreed to a time-share arrangement in much the same way as divorced parents do with their children. The dogs spend their nights at her place and their days at mine. I keep the three cats and the furniture we shared for six years that the cats destroyed. We split the costs of a helper who stays with the kids in the daytime and looks after them when we travel. Gabriella asked if I would mind keeping the cats, including Giorgio, at my place forever, so she could buy an Eames Lounge chair and Ottoman for her apartment that they couldn't destroy.

So many cats fall from balconies and windows, vets have a name for the phenomenon. *High Rise Syndrome* was coined by a New York vet in 1976 whose practice saw around 150 flying cats each year. "The distance cats have fallen and survived is nothing short of amazing" he wrote. "Our record heights for survival are as follows: 18 stories onto a hard surface (concrete, asphalt, dirt, car roof), 20 stories onto shrubbery and 28 stories onto a canopy or awning".[1]

Ten years later, two vets in New York City studied the injuries of 132 cats that had fallen out of buildings. Ninety percent of all cats treated survived their falls. What was really strange was that the incidence of mortality and injury peaked at the seven story mark. Only 5% of cats that fell from anywhere higher than the seventh story died, but 10% of cats that fell from between the second to the sixth story died. Incredibly, cats that fell from much higher stories sustained injuries no worse than those that fell from the seventh story. In fact, the chances they suffered any kind of fracture actually diminished. The cats that sustained the worst injuries were those that had fallen the shortest distances. Most cats that fell from the seventh or eighth story suffered a broken bone. Only one cat out of thirteen that fell from the ninth story or higher suffered a broken bone. The cat that fell from the 32nd floor of an apartment onto concrete was released from hospital two days later with a chipped tooth and a mild case of pneumothorax (collapsed lung). He turned out to be fine.[2]

Giorgio, like all cats that fall, owes his life to his evolutionary biology, physiology and a phenomenon called Aerial Righting Reflex, shared by all animals that live in trees. It's sad to think that Giorgio has never even *seen* a tree, much less climbed one but that is not material here. Or maybe it is. If he had more climbing experience perhaps he'd be more agile. Or at least have a healthier respect for risk.

1   Robinson, Gordon W. "The High Rise Trauma Syndrome in Cats", *Feline Practice*, Sep. 1976: 40-43, 41. Print.
2   Whitney, Wayne O. and Mehlhaff, Cheryl J. "High Rise Syndrome in Cats," *JAVMA*. Nov. 1987: 1399-1403. Print.

In free fall, cats use their eyes and inner ears to help them determine which way is up (or down) and this lets them position themselves during a fall so they reduce the force of impact. The cat's head rotates first, and then its spine follows, allowing its rear feet to align with its front feet as it soars through the air. Once righted, the cat splays its limbs outwards and arches its back, slowing the fall even further, and ensuring it lands on its feet.[3] Landing on their feet provides a much safer landing than landing on their backs or another part of their body. This explains why cats that fall from lower floors tend to end up with worse injuries than those that fall from higher floors: they don't get time to right themselves.

Humans don't fare nearly as well as cats when they fall from buildings. That's because an average-sized man in free fall experiences a terminal velocity or maximum speed of 120 miles an hour. A falling cat's terminal velocity is only 60 miles an hour.[4] Humans tend to land on their feet or their heads, compounding the risk of injury. It is rare that a human survives a fall more than six stories onto concrete, and even then his injuries are likely to be critical. It is rare for a cat to die from a fall of anything up to 30 stories.

My apartment in Hong Kong is on the fourth floor of a low-rise block. I only learned this recently but four turns out to be an unlucky number in Chinese. The word for four sounds like the word for death. Many buildings in Singapore and Hong Kong don't even have a fourth floor. I also learned recently that my balcony has railings just wide enough for a cat to slip through. A couple of days before Giorgio's fall, I spotted him squeezing through the railings and sitting on the three inch wide strip of concrete outside the balcony, looking back at me, making sure I had seen him. I got up and went straight to the kitchen and opened a tin of cat food. Within seconds he was safely back inside, and the balcony door was locked. The next day, I went looking for some green gauze, the kind they sell in garden shops, to cat proof the balcony. I looked around and asked a few people, and made a couple of phone calls, but no one seemed to know where to find that kind of thing. And then I got distracted and forgot.

---

3   Diamond, Jared. "Why Cats have Nine Lives," *Nature*, Vol 332. Apr. 1988: 586-7. Print.
4   Whitney and Mehlhaff.

Two nights later I got home from work to find two cats reclining on the sofa next to our helper, and three dogs asleep on the rug in front of the TV. Everyone was watching Project Runway, or Project Runaway as our helper thinks it's called. Our helper left, and I closed the balcony door, checking as I always do that no cat was hiding under one of the outdoor chairs. I had a shower, poured myself a glass of wine and started thinking about what I could defrost for dinner when it occurred to me I hadn't seen Giorgio.

I opened a tin of food and called his name. Everyone ran towards me but Giorgio. A feeling of doom began to knot inside my gut. If he wasn't inside the apartment, and he wasn't on the balcony, there was only one place he could be.

I threw on some shoes and raced downstairs. Gabriella was travelling for work and wouldn't be home for another four weeks, as tends to happen in times of crisis. I crept through the car park whispering his name. Underneath my balcony is the floor of a metal car stacker, a device popular in space-poor Hong Kong that allows two cars to be parked in a single spot. The floor of the stacker sits about six feet off the ground and is made from thick corrugated iron. If he had fallen, he must have hit the car stacker and bounced off.

Whichever way he landed he was likely to be in shock. There is a wall behind the car park and I hitched myself up on top of it, walked along it tentatively because I, unlike my cat have long passed the age where I get a thrill from walking along thin ledges, twelve feet off the ground. I called his name and I heard a noise. It sounded like a sick baby.

I jumped down from the wall, lay on my stomach on the floor of the car park, and looked under the belly of the only parked car. Stuck in its middle was Giorgio, his white body covered in blood and soot and his eyes clamped shut. I tried to coax him out but he refused to budge. I tried to slide underneath the car but the chassis was too low to the ground. The only way to get him was to stretch my arm in as far as it would go, pinch the scruff of his neck between my fingers and drag him out. I carried him upstairs in my arms, horrified by his floppy body and the blood and bruising on his face.

I found my wallet and keys and ran out into the street and flagged a taxi. We got inside, Giorgio emitting a barely audible croak as I told the driver to take us to Mongkok, the only place in Hong Kong I knew to have a 24-hour animal clinic. I didn't know where it was, but I remembered its name: Peace Avenue Vet clinic. If the driver could find Peace Avenue, and Giorgio could keep himself alive until we got there, maybe he would survive his second fall.

Taxis in Hong Kong's New Territories present a challenge to the non-Cantonese speaking passenger. My driver knew I wanted to go to Mongkok, but "Peace Avenue" in English meant nothing to him. I kicked myself for wasting five years in Hong Kong when I should have been learning Cantonese. I slumped back into my seat and felt my heart thrash inside my chest like a freshly caught fish inside a bucket.

Apart from a couple of large arterial roads that slice through its middle, most of the streets in Mongkok are gnarled and crooked and crammed with cars and people. The last time I was here was a year earlier with a small group of MFA students, doing an exercise on immersion writing. We wandered through a food market, pens and notebooks in our hands. It was raining hard and we stopped underneath the awning of a butcher's shop. Knotted sheep's intestines hung from hooks under red lamp shades, and a fresh pig's head stared out at the street from an inside counter. The lone vegetarian, I stood back, feeling sad for the pig, rain splashing the legs of my jeans.

We were interrupted by a loud crash that sounded like part of a building collapsing. Walking towards the noise we discovered a middle-aged man sprawled out on the ground in front of a woman selling folding umbrellas. He had jumped out the window of his apartment and crashed landed on the awning above a fruit stall. An older man kneeled over him. The jumper lifted himself up slowly, waving the older man away. Cursing, he looked down at his soaked trousers and limped back inside the narrow hallway to his building. His life had been spared by an awning, now crumpled with a tear down its middle, resting on a stack of empty fruit boxes. An ambulance pulled up and a crowd gathered, heads up, in spite of the rain, looking at the side of the building for clues. There were six stories, but it was impossible he had fallen so far. More likely to have been from the third floor, the only apartment with an open window. The crowd disappeared and all that was left was an angry fruit stall owner, shouting at the ambulance men in their plastic gloves, pointing at his broken awning.

My taxi crawled up and down Peace Avenue through gridlocked traffic. Eventually, the driver stopped and pointed to a distant sign that said 24 Hour Vet, and I, worrying that Giorgio might not survive another trip around the block, and if he did that I probably would not, thanked the driver, gave him a big tip, and jumped out of his cab.

"My cat fell six stories!" I shouted, pushing to the front of the counter of what turned out to be Peace Avenue Veterinary Clinic. Hyperbole helps in an emergency, or at least that has been my experience in life to date. "Room five," the receptionist said, waving at a room behind her. "You can take him in now."

"Another flying cat" the vet said with an Australian drawl, coaxing Giorgio out of his cat carrier. He checked him over quickly before deciding Giorgio's jaw, spine and legs would need to be x-rayed and an ultrasound taken of his internal organs. "He's landed on his jaw and that's never a good thing" he said. Whatever the results, Giorgio would need to spend a couple of days in intensive care so his pain could be managed. The first 72 hours after a fall were critical and he needed to be monitored. "Is he going to be ok?" I asked, as a vet nurse started blotting the muck off Giorgio's face. "Too soon to tell," he said. I kissed Giorgio goodbye and walked out into the dirty Mongkok rain with my empty cat carrier.

I went home and spent most of the night Googling "cats that fall from buildings". The next morning I called in sick to work. I have a boring job in human resources and the last thing I felt like facing was people. At ten o'clock the vet called. Giorgio had sustained multiple fractures to his jaw and his right front leg. His jaw required immediate surgery. He would be anesthetized and wire and concrete used to rebuild his jaw. It would take at least three weeks for the concrete to set, maybe even longer, during which time he would need to be fed through a tube. A hole would be made in his esophagus so the tube could be inserted into his stomach. Feeding would need to be done manually, by me, every three hours, around the clock.

Giorgio spent a week in intensive care. I went to visit him on his second day in hospital. That was a mistake. He looked like a monster with a thick plastic collar, pillars pressing his jaws open, his thick white coat stained brown by drool. He stared through me with glazed red eyes, not even registering as I tried to stroke the top of his nose. On my way home I rang Gabriella who had just landed in London. "He looks terrible," I said. "Maybe we should think about putting him down." "No!" she said and I agreed. In the space of six months, I had lost her and Filippo. I couldn't afford to lose anyone else. I was running out of things to love.

Giorgio was released from hospital. I arranged with my boss to work half days in the office and half days from home for the next fortnight so I could perform the duties of cat carer. My boss, who knows me as a middle-aged woman without children or a partner, shot me a look. All I could do was raise my eyebrows, exhale and say, "I know."

The vet suggested I buy a cage so the other cats and dogs would not get the chance to rip out Giorgio's feeding tube. I positioned the cage in the middle of the lounge room so he could see everything around him, and filled it with my old t-shirts. For three weeks, I fed him every three hours. When I wasn't feeding him, I was changing his bandages, or cleaning his cage, or administering drugs, or stroking his nose while we waited for the painkillers to kick in, or listening to him wail from the pain and discomfort of a mouth forced open with wire and concrete. Every three days we returned to the vet for a checkup. His progress seemed minimal. His weight had been five kilos before the accident and now it was half that. The bandage that held his tube in place wore through the skin and an infection formed. More drugs, more dressings, more stress. Sleep deprived, towards the end of his third week at home, I had a flash one night of taking him back to the vet that very instant and having him put down. Instead I pulled the pillow over my head and tried to suffocate myself. It's harder than you think.

He's back home now, out of the cage, minus his tube and his Queen Elizabeth collar, with a gaping hole in his neck that looks like he wandered into the path of a stray bullet. He needs to relearn how to eat. Last night, despite his broken leg, which requires a further surgery when we've both recovered from this one, he hopped up onto my bed and folded himself into my arms. For the first time in four weeks he nuzzled his head into my chest and purred. I stroked the spot under his chin until we both fell asleep.

All travel and social activities have been suspended for the past four weeks. My days have been filled with me trundling off to work in a fog after a sleepless night, racing back home and attending to my sick cat. The vet bills have so far amounted to a week's salary, with more to come. But he is my cat and I would pay anything I can to make him better. That, I suppose, makes me a cat person: a cat person who will never again allow the door to her balcony to be opened until her lease runs out and she finds a new apartment somewhere on the ground floor.

KEEGAN LESTER

THE TOPOGRAPHY OF
MOUNTAINS BEYOND MOUNTAINS

Remember the world after reading Paul Farmer's biography?
That we thought it could be saved with a Ph.D. in anthropology?
Edith, remember when we realized we could do the same thing
by hugging strangers at the end of the bar? I never left that bar.
I closed that bar down, slept in the backroom on a pile of cardboard
next to a mop. The ammonia smell made me think about hospitals.
I've never trusted doctors, the thumping in their stethoscope ears
or Ohio. Last winter I chucked so much wood, a lesser man
would have blushed, by which I mean your father. By which I mean
I made your father blush because of my brute strength and ability
to grow a mustache. People are not supposed to look directly into
the moon, but I don't believe in that shit. I think that this is America
and we should have the right to praise any damn thing we want,
and I only pray during football season and the moon is the
best wing man I've ever had. It helped me land you once,
twice and I'm betting the odds on a third time. It's us against the world
the moon told me one night, through its Swiss Cheese mouth
the way you might expect John Wayne to, before taking a blank
to the stomach. Before his tiny ketchup boot prints stained the set.

DOMESTICS & ACCIDENTS
A Roadmap

i.
Some words are pebbles
and old grass.
Some fill the room like a road.

ii.
I press your words into maps.
Fold them so your chest bends
and the road runs through you.

iii.
At night I leave
our sleeping children in the yard
so I can run the road across their backs.
So I can be childless and dark.

iv.
I gravel up
at the shoulder.
Never go anywhere.

v.
If the world stopped spinning
we would all be heavy and seasick.
Then it wouldn't be just me.

vi.
The road makes a sound
like everything is coming
and then it's gone.
Sometimes I do.

JAMES D'AGOSTINO

THE SUPERIOR INTERIOR TEMPORAL GYRUS

is my name for the tricked out
van I am never going
to own. I know it. Though

it's also the name
for the part of the brain
that spikes in activity

right before you
get a metaphor or joke
or bright idea. I know

the fog is not the day's main
deal so this mist is just its
side thing, but

very little else. I'm supposed to
know Thoreau, but I'm on
a little roll, so

fuck the huckleberry and his pond
light. Night we got married
our friends got kicked

out of there, MA midsummer,
90 at night, green flies want
knife fights, guests want

squid ink lobster ravioli
and I want you
to know on the night

I finally use one full tree's
worth of matchsticks,
I'll turn to you and not

when I came to die discover
I had not or at least
where you were when

the lights went out.

LEIGH BENNETT

WHIP

Tommy had never made a pie, but today, for Clementine, he would. He'd scour the pantry for ingredients and bake the perfect pie for Clem. Flavor was first, so he combed through the dog-eared pages of his mother's recipe book, flimsy and sticky with love. Blueberry, strawberry, raspberry. How many times had he and Clem foraged the wild pickings from her backyard vines, the bright red juices dripping down the chin of her seedy smile? But it wasn't quite season. He considered a pie in her name. Was there such a thing as a Clementine pie? If so, surely he'd tasted it and couldn't remember. But how bitter it would be, and peeling the skins would take an hour, at least. He needed to work faster.

He knew Clem's secrets—the fights at home, that scar from the old hickory grove, that she still took her pills mashed in applesauce—and yearned for the ones he knew he could never know—the touch of her polished fingertips, the delicate curves of her back. But Tommy couldn't, for the life of him, remember Clem's favorite pie, and in his excitement, had forgotten to ask. He'd always loved Ma's Thanksgiving pecan, but it was June and this wasn't about what *he* wanted. Key lime, sugar, blackberry, chocolate? Shoofly would make a mess; cream seemed too obvious.

He settled on lemon meringue—the picture in the recipe book an echo of Clem's yellow-white hair—then set out for the parts: flour, white sugar, cornstarch, eggs, butter, and lemons. Of course lemons—tart and bright, juiced and zested, boiled and whipped into foam. He'd use one of Ma's frozen crusts, the ones she'd been saving for the church bake sale, because the crust, the crust didn't matter. Only the soft whisked billows of tangy meringue.

He laid the pieces on the counter while his parents slept, and saw the sun come into the small room where he and Clem watched *I Love Lucy* after school. Sometimes his dad's old Magnavox scrambled the picture or the wicker chairs scratched their backs; that's when they'd sit in the grass and tell stories or flick lizards from the patio screen.

The pie was taking shape now before him, and each new step, each ingredient, he handled with care. Because a pie is a tricky thing, fragile and sweet; because you never know if you're doing it right until it's done. But when it was done, the peaks pricked up in perfect curls, and Tommy felt proud. He wrapped the pie in cardboard and tied it with a bow. Outside, he rolled out his bicycle, same as every day, and headed for school, the pie perched on his fingertips like an offering.

The hallways were empty for homeroom and Tommy was late. The ride had taken longer than he thought, always stopping to resettle the pie. Ma would scold him for sure, but he felt too happy to care. He made his way to Clem's locker where he stood and waited. He waited by Clem's locker where he knew she would appear in a moment—knowing her every move or sensing it.

When the bell sounded, the hallway filled, and Tommy dragged the thin bow between his fingers—prolonging the gift. He lifted the pie from its home and held it before him, taking in the last whiff of lemon, the zip of rind, the final picture of success.

Then he saw her, rounding the corner in the crowd, her books stacked neatly under her bare, scarred arm. She was giggling and gossiping.

It took her a moment to notice him there—the boy with the pie at her locker—and in that moment, he launched his attack. The pie slapped Clem's face with a THWACK.

Lemon. Meringue. Fear.

Curd covered her shoulders and speckled her hair (the exact color of her hair), crust stuck in clumps to her shirt. For a second he considered running, but only for a second. Instead, he stood frozen, all eyes but Clem's on him.

When the tin slid down the base of her chin, Tommy saw

the shock in Clem's eyes, wide with cream, dripping with confusion.

Clem scowled. Clem glared. They all scowled. They all glared.

The bell rang again and the crowds thinned, full enough on gossip for first period. Clementine gathered her books, leaned into Tommy, and whispered *thank you*, licking the thick whip from her parted lips.

OPEN SEASON

I get all my news from the weather report or
I get all my weather from my news feed or
windows refuse to tell me what I wanna know.
Beat cops & Freedom Tower & Mobil sign

& "Zero Viz," the song that gets the last
laugh. Ha, ho, oh, I'm gonna get curtains one
of these storms & I am going to get down
from here one of these days. The season

between Sandy & Nemo, three months of
sandbagged nesting & now we use hot breath
& the flats of our fists to make animal tracks.
We weren't bombed out, we were bombed in.

Calling all groundhogs, calling all perennials,
all you strange herds & goodhearts, come on.

ANNIE GUTHRIE

*THE ORACLE

sometimes shadow becomes articulate

eyes that have the world,

looking, there is a splinter
broken off inside

("my sight")

what doubt can be in eyes that have the world, you
in them–?

*THE GOSSIP

I don't always want what we have, she is saying.

He is silent. Outside, dark clouds, fish hopping, tilling waves

back from shore. Sometimes more is happening, he says, finally.

The sun's coming up, she says. *Look at the light that's kept.*

I'd like to keep it up, he says.

She is silent, tilling shore back from shore.

Don't make apart what is otherwise the same, he says, finally.

What. she says.

Never try & stare darkness in the face, he says, darkening.

DMITRY BORSHCH

About the Artwork

The following four ink and paper drawings were created by Dmitry Borshch as part of the series *Exiled From Truth: Nine Allegories*. The series continues to develop, and the pieces are united by color, style, and technique. Borshch says, "Allegory, drawn or written, is a product of that mind which regards truth as existing-in-absence: it does exist yet is absent from our view. Allegories like mine would not be needed if truth were openly present."

The Artist Speaks On "The Making of Brothers"

"This drawing is an allegorical interpretation of the ceremony of adelphopoiesis, which I translate as 'the making of brothers', hence the drawing's name. I started drawing it in ninety-eight simply as a ceremonial double portrait with a reptile; two Polish youngsters posed for this as yet unnamed ceremony during one afternoon. Unsure of the ceremony's name and purpose, I left the drawing unfinished for about five months. When something reminded me of adelphopoiesis, which I read about in the book called 'Same-Sex Unions in Premodern Europe', probably in late ninety-five, I rushed to finish the drawing. It was finished in January of last year and is about forty-two by thirty-seven inches. The reptile, which could be a crocodile or an alligator, symbolizes homoerotic yearning."

Notes on "Betrothal of the Virgins"

The word on male figure's cap reads "groom," and the word on the female figure's cap reads "bride."

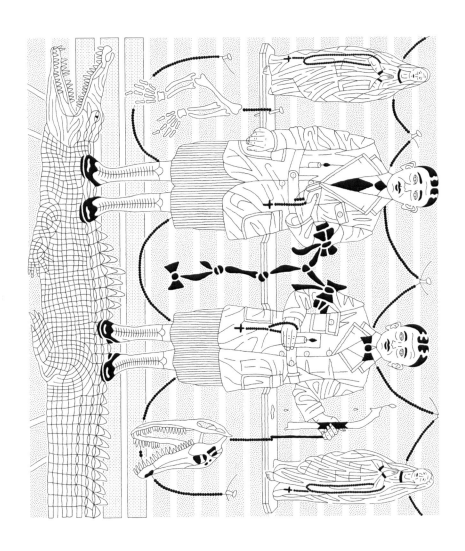

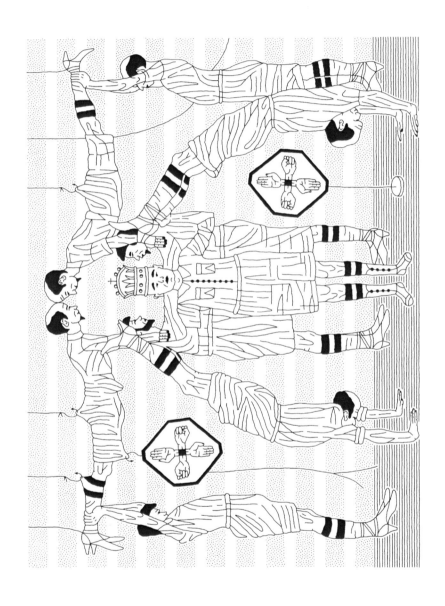

Nikola Tesla in the Bears' Dream

He moved like a puppet
in an experimental film
shorn over
with the greys
of some late country
crippled with blood
belt-sanded, as if only bits
of him could be held in time.
The bear regarded him
and pawed behind
his great brown ear.
Whatever Nikola Tesla said
was lost in the sounds
of the bear breathing.
He didn't seem to know
he was in a dream, but
not the subject of that dream,
and gave a yelp when
from the bone-white architecture
of birches came one
after another bear, exactly
alike, and none of them seeing
each other except the one
who dreamed it. He (that
dreaming bear) made
a low growl and touched
their fur with his fur. He
ran down his claws among it,
but none felt. Tesla in the dream
thought: how like life. He thought:
how like it, indeed. He flickered
in and elsewhere.

81

The bear slept a long time.
Tesla began to dance
& to the bear it seemed he might
be caught in a web, or flying
drunk on wrong fruit.

HISHAM BUSTANI
Translated by Thoraya El-Rayyes

[APOCALYPSE NOW]

Originally published in Arabic:
The Perception of Meaning (Beirut: Dar al-Adab, 2012)

1

Because you are
alone,
and because life is a building seventy stories high,
you couldn't but embrace the air,
you couldn't but leave your memories scattered on the pavement in a pool
of red,
and so...
you jumped.

2

The boat that crossed the river did not find a happy ending.

The trees casting shadows over the water were adorned with rotting corpses.
The leaves drowned in the smell of everpresent death. Through them pro-
truded faces, camouflaged.
"Don't any of you play chess?" yelled the commander. But the row of pawns
had just been met with the gush of machine guns fired fast, and vaporized
into the sky.
No knights here, and the castles are ruins with broken windows, and as
soon as the commander went down to inspect the site, he was blown up by
a landmine.

The boat that crossed the river did not find a happy ending.
At the moment it arrived at the end of its long journey, it turned round and
went back, with no passengers.

3

Apes do not wage wars.
Apes do not invent instruments of torture.
Apes do not puncture the ozone with fossil fuels.
"Humans are descended from apes?"
Who says the apes would approve?

When Man climbed the tree to meet his ancestors, all the leaves fell and species vanished. No colour but washed-out grey, and no sound but the breaking of branches in his clumsy hands. Before a full white moon, he sat on one of the branches and began to cry.

4

The bull that just got a cleaver to the neck,
filled his jowls with laughter,
and strode vainly between the soldiers.

"We have trained young men to drop bombs on people, but their commanders won't allow them to write fuck on their airplanes because it is obscene…"

The bull does not know the word fuck,
nor does he know how to drop bombs on anyone.
That is why he walked, and laughed, in the midst of the fire.

5

The peasant, whose petrol-soaked clothes caught a spark, dissolved immediately into the soil in a flare of celebration.

Part of him became flowers, part of him became migrating birds. Only his heart went on pulsing within the earth, leaving behind seisms and volcanoes.

6

The murderer walking down the street was followed by his victims.

He swats them away but they do not go. He runs far from them, only making them stick closer.

Only when a bullet came to him from the top of a derelict building did he sleep in peace, then wake up and join their protest that ends at the horizon.

7
The orange man walks, trudging
guzzling with his broom, thousands of people's vomit,
at night after he sleeps –
he is visited by a single dream/nightmare:

The broom grows and grows and grows,
its bristles strike like hurricanes and send flying the city of exhaust fumes
and polystyrene boxes.

And when he is awoken by a mouse moving in his stomach,
he runs to the bathroom,
out of his guts emerge gas stations, opposition parties, fast-food restaurants,
newspapers, shopping malls and neighbourhoods stagnant with featureless
inhabitants.
And before the water current that sweeps it all away stops, he throws himself in so that he might die.
But he finds himself -again and again- in the street,
walking, trudging,
guzzling with his broom, thousands of people's vomit.

8
Winter:
nature's flagellant.
She wears grey and cries over her choices.
She lightning whips herself and screams thunder and tears amass.
Winter: nature's lament at losing her first deep, she tries to flood and is not
able. For he who emerged from her water once upon a chance has built
dams, diverted rivers and dug gigantic reservoirs underground.
Nature tries to flood and is not able.
Tears of joy? She will cry tears of joy when we part one day, but we survive
and she withers.

Cry, cry, said Man. I will bottle your sorrow and sell it.

9
Behold the flowers sprawled out over the fields:
white, red, yellow, lavender.
How naïve,
they do not know the concrete is coming.

10

He sees them darting through the streets as if bitten by a serpent.
Addicted to devastation, their bodies object, so what do they do?

The molar objects: they extract it.
The gallbladder objects: they excise it.

They congregate like the dead at the gates of eternity. Above the gate, a sign:
Brains Excised Here.

11

The White God cruises across the river of bare-assed savages with opera
music.
From the long chimney emerge Verde, Caruso, Rossini and Wagner.

The White God wants to cross the mountain on his floating phonograph, so
he opened a gaming hall for them:
They drank whiskey, played poker and their drool flowed onto the strippers'
podium.
The White God taught them his intoxicating miracles, so they carried the
floating phonograph to where trees patiently await their killer. They were
slaughtered by slanted lines across their trunks that meet in the center, then
their blood was gathered to be sent to the Old World and return as radiant
junk.
As for the opera, it still warbles out of the speakers of bomber airplanes and
the tears of the trees.

12

"Kill a man and you're a murderer
Kill many and you're a conqueror
Kill them all, you're a God."
So said Dave Mustaine in his sharp voice and walked off.

Mr. Anderson decided to be a God, and so he flooded Bopal with a present in the form of a poisonous cloud of pesticide and enclosed a personally signed card: "Courtesy of Union Carbide."

The deaths—unfortunately for Mr. Anderson—only numbered fifteen thousand.

"Don't leave loose ends" he used to yell at them. But they did not perfect their task: they forgot to fix a bullet in the forehead of every corpse and some of the dead continued to live. For this, his assistants were sentenced to jail for two years and fined 2,500 dollars.

As for him, he returned like the conquerors wreathed in bay leaves, to his birthplace in Bridgehampton-Long Island, where he takes his Chihuahua on a daily walk to breathe in the clean air of what was once the lands of the Shinnecock, listening to the echo of fishermen choking to death- those killed by Mr. Anderson Senior with a poisonous cloud of smallpox.

"Ten thousand… Fifteen thousand… How many generations will it take for Mr. Anderson to become a God? We've had no luck this millennium" he thought, as his grandson Mr. Anderson Junior played with an aircraft carrier in the swimming pool.

"Eureka" yelled the grandson jumping out of the water, and immediately sent them bottles swaying like women filled with his intoxicating liquid. And as they greedily gulp it down, fantasies of a new world fizz up into their brains so they die at once and are resurrected as slaves in front of a throne veiled by a screen of liquid crystal.

"Kill them all, you're a God! " chuckled Mr. Anderson, "What does it make me then, if I resurrect them as slaves?"

Dave Mustaine could not find an answer to this question. So, he breaks his electric guitar onstage every day and raises his middle finger in the audience's face.

13
The naï-playing dervish who emerged from the pen of Nâzim Hekmat and played a world of clouds, beautiful women and defeated villains could not endure the rebounding echo of his melodies, for he was barricaded between rivers of tar and concrete dams.

The cypress he sat under groaned, and so he came to break his naï into small wooden pieces and scatter them into the air so that they would not be music after today.

14
The handsome whale, Tilikum.
They stole him from his ocean and crammed him into a fish tank.
And when he drowned his trainer in protest,
he was at once transformed into material for news broadcasts.
Chewed between newscasters' teeth and swallowed,
to provide their daily allowance
of Omega-3.

15
Birds of a feather fall together.

Birds of a feather.
Fall together.

Birds.
Of.
A.
Feather.
Fall.
Together.

He finished reciting his favorite song.
Folded his hunting rifle over his arm, and turned to head back.
Behind him small corpses were trembling over the wide plain,
then fell still, to be consumed by the sun and flies.

16

The whispers of the dead.
He stood, listening.

"A kerosene heater and seven of us in a small room. The cold strangled us with our breath."
"Two speeding lights, then cold metal ripped me off the face of the earth and put me inside it."
"I lived in a house that floated on the water, then it decided to dive."
"I am seven years old. A smart bomb found its way into our neighbourhood."
"I am three months old. A rubber bullet found its way into my head."
"I was still swimming in warm fluid when my mother got a baton to her swollen stomach."

When the voices went quiet – despite the sun beating above his head and people passing before him quickly in their cars – he realized that he was in a hole, and began to whisper.

17
To Sayyed Banat (Abul Fida)

No, a full moon did not mark the day of your birth.
No, a cloud did not cast you in shadow wherever you placed your feet.
No, you were not the Seal of the Prophets nor did you bring forth a Book.

All there is to it is that a city belching smoke and clatter kidnapped you
from between your mother's thighs and force-fed you her sour milk- that
you vomited time after time- then carried your gauntness and cast it on her
sidewalk:
loose cigarettes, sleight of hand tricks, books on the torment of the grave
and toothpicks.

At night, you dance like a traffic light possessed by madness until you col-
lapse from delusion.

And when you awake after much sweat:
The city is laughing and laughing, rolling left and right on her back and
over on her stomach.
"Is it you who denounces me?" she says, releasing her mice and her odors
like the slashes of a whipmaster on your back.

But you are stubborn: you get skinnier, and the city grows paunchier along
with its liars.

On the bed of the poor hospital, he crumbled without a single person to his
side and disappeared into forgetting.

18

Suddenly, while some slept in business class seats like children in their mothers' bosoms, it opened its mouth and screamed.
It was not a regular scream, an enormous cloud of dust emerged with it.

Airlines were paralyzed, and the business class passengers were enraged to have their colored lollipops snatched away.
"This is a catastrophe…" they yelled, then held a meeting in the top floor of a skyscraper and found the solution.

After they fastened the gigantic stopper and pushed it firmly into the hole, champagne corks went flying and out gushed –strangely enough– a fiery red liquid, in spite of the ice. The liquid was called: lava. It's temperature: 700-1200 degrees Celsius. After cooling, it turns into a type of basalt suitable for determining the age of the earth.

As for the passengers in business class, they dissolved completely. In billions of years, other beings- smarter than we are- will not find their fossils.

19
When he places his hand on the big button and the glass light moves horizontally, the forest groans.

Here is the tree's finger pulled along plastic wheels through tight corridors to come out through the side opening. Aah... a photocopying mistake, he throws it in the trash can.

Let's try again. The tree's foot this time. Her head. Her hips. Her trunk. He throws it all away angrily: "It's one of those days." And the photocopying machine gets jammed with every push of the button.

Months ago, she was magnificent, spreading green in the air, seducing the birds. Today, her body parts lay dismembered/ pulverized/ bleached in the trash can.

***

Endnotes

2
The **boat** travels down the river in Francis Ford Coppola's film *Apocalypse Now,* a reinterpretation of Conrad's *Heart of Darkness.*

4
The slain **bull** and the **quote** from Francis Ford Coppola's film *Apocalypse Now* a reinterpretation of Conrad's *Heart of Darkness.*

5
In memory of the Korean **peasant,** Lee Kyoung Hae, who died in protest against the World Trade Organization summit in Mexico in 2003.

11
Fitzcarraldo was not an *opera* lover, he was a rubber baron with an army of 5,000 men who carved out a piece of land in South America the size of Belgium for himself. But the German director Werner Herzog did not see a story in that! The baron dismantled a ship and transported it over a mountain, and the Europeans built an opera house in the Amazon. Now that's a story! Thus, the lying white movie with a mongrel plot came to be.

The *crying tree*: The meaning of the word "cahuchu" which is an indigenous South American name for the rubber tree.

12
Dave Mustaine: A singer/songwriter and founder of the American rock band Megadeth. The opening quote is taken from the lyrics of the song Captive Honour which is in fact a quote from the French biologist and philosopher Jean Rostand (1894 – 1977).

Mr. Anderson: Warren Anderson is a former Chairman and Chief Executive Officer of the American company Union Carbide whose pesticide factory in Bopal, India leaked poisonous gas on December 3rd 1984- killing 15,000 people as well as injuring and disfiguring tens of thousands of others.

The Shinnecock: An indigenous American tribe from Long Island, New York. The men of the tribe were skilled fishermen and sailors, and many were exterminated by viruses brought by the white man from Europe.

13
Nâzim Hekmat (1902 – 1963): The well-known Turkish writer and poet. He spent twenty six years (between 1925 and 1951) in and out of jail because of his communist activism and spent the rest of his life in exile. He wrote about the dervish in a story called "The Loving Cloud", published for the first time in 1962.

18
On Sunday 21st April 2010, a volcano which had been dormant for two hundred years erupted in south Iceland, creating a one kilometer long fissure in a glacial ice sheet and emitting a cloud of dust that halted air travel in Europe for days, costing airlines billions of dollars in losses.

***

Translator's note: This translation was carried out in collaboration with the author. Several minor edits from the original Arabic text were made in order to preserve the musicality of the original text, these have been approved by the author.

DILLON J. WELCH

CATCHING UP

Ode to the expertly eyeballed teaspoon.
To what we're left with: unequal
servings. Ode to the impossible
us, glancing silence like a reused
sieve. To reconnecting. To the old
me, in swim trunks and wrestling
a fish to the deck. To memories!
To dead fish! Ode to our bodies
alive as they are. To the cliff
one of us will empty the other
off of, the day of untimely dismissal.
Our tiny pieces spelling some breezy shape
some feet above water. Ode to commitment
in wind. To the beautiful behaviors
of ocean rocks. How they tumble uneven
in the turning current. Ode to movement, impulsive
transportation, leaving here
to end up there, unfazed. The choice
to bike down the skinniest hallway.
Ode to goldenrod and misquoting yourself
beneath a checkered awning. To Parameters.
Stencil-thin screen doors and backyards
best used for family gatherings. Ode
to gathering families. To you, Elizabeth,
and your failure to comment, again
on the garden.

CLARITY
Youngstown, Ohio

"You know the one about your father
and Channel 33?" I'm nineteen, I shake my head. "Okay,
so thirty years ago, VCR's got big
and adult videos came out. We got the A/B switches—
you've seen them in the rooms—B for cable and A for the porn
that loops every couple of hours. The hotel
up the road got them—it's business,
what can you do? All right—
so 33 comes into the office
and says they want to do an interview. It was just a reporter,
a cameraman, and your father." My uncle focuses
as if he's reciting a prayer
to the key rack. The phone rings. He writes a name
on a scrap of paper, jabs it
through a key hook, hangs up
and says "So the reporter asks your father,
'Do you get complaints about the videos?'
Your father rubs his beard—
he's nervous—looks into the camera
and says, 'Yes—sometimes
customers call the office
and complain that the picture
isn't clear enough.'"

THE COMEDIENNE

Pauline thought up her best material on the subway, and scribbled ideas into the four-inch Wexford notebook she kept in the back pocket of her jeans. Later, alone in her house, she'd get out the notes and pace the dining room, try to turn whatever fleeting amusement she thought up on the D Train into an actual joke. That spring, her best bits were about Lucas, her lover, and so, while she could practice them at home, make herself laugh wildly into the bathroom mirror, they weren't useful beyond the vinyl sided walls of her own isolation. She couldn't very well go on stage and admit to having an extramarital affair—not unless she wanted to be found out. At first, she tried to contort the jokes so that they were about someone else—her husband, her brother-in-law—but it never worked. Jokes about Lucas were only really funny in the context of Pauline's bad decision to have started sleeping with him in the first place. When she wasn't wandering her house laughing about it, it kept her up at night.

Pauline was thirty-four and had never lived anywhere except New York. In addition to her affair with Lucas, she had an overweight Persian cat named Mr. Face and a burgeoning career as a stand-up comic and a wobbly marriage to a man named Drew, who was a scientist. He had been away since January.

The trouble in Pauline's marriage was like this: When Drew had taken a two-year appointment at the University of Kentucky, Pauline refused to move. She'd never so much as *entertained* the thought of living in a small southern city, and Drew was *well aware* of Pauline's plans and values when they got married four years ago. Los Angeles, maybe, but Kentucky? No. But this job was the best thing Drew could do professionally. He was passionate about his work.

So, after a lot of deliberating and pleading and finally compromising—sort of—they now had that rare and precarious species of marriage: long distance. They'd agreed it was a temporary arrangement, but was two years really temporary? Drew's position was the kind that would lead to other, better paid but similarly located positions later on; that was why it was so lucrative. They were always talking about it that way: *The Position.* Pauline thought it an apt word, given the way Drew's work seemed, lately, to turn him in the wrong direction. His ideas about life—where to live, and why to live there—were shifting for circumstances Pauline was loathe to acknowledge; she felt a slow tide pulling her life away.

She wanted Drew. She wanted to be a professional comic. Now it looked as though she couldn't have both, so she buoyed herself on bad decisions: staying up all night, sleeping with Lucas, eating too many pancakes.

The Position was grant-funded research on bed bugs; Drew's recent studies suggested that kidney bean leaves, which were covered with microscopic hook hairs, attracted—through scent or something—the pests, and then trapped and killed them in the leaves' sharp fur. This was not, in fact, a new finding, but rather, confirmation of the effectiveness of a folk remedy that had been common in Eastern Europe until the introduction of strong pesticides in the 1950s. Pauline's comedy, which was almost always autobiographical in nature, included a joke about this, about the fact that her husband was paid to do field work running experiments that old Estonian women had already proven successful a century ago. "This is what counts as a scientific breakthrough these days!" she'd tell her audience, who were already slapping their thighs at her impression of an old Estonian woman. It was a very good bit.

On Essex Street, orange light came through the wide restaurant windows, made the crowded dining room cozy. Lucas ordered the fried-chicken sandwich. Again.

"How can you keep eating that?" Pauline asked.

"They don't start serving lunch until 11:30," he said. It was 10:45. "But they like me, so they make an exception." He spoke with his mouth full. It was a bad habit, a disgusting thing that Pauline's parents hadn't tolerated. During Pauline's childhood, rude mealtime behavior resulted in being sent to sit on the basement steps until everyone else—Pauline's parents, grandparents, sister, and often, sad, unmarried Uncle Gino—finished their own meals. Afterwards, Pauline was ushered to the kitchen to help with the mountainous sink of dishes. She was permitted to finish her own plate—which her mother had Saran-wrapped and refrigerated—once clean up was complete. Thinking of this, Pauline felt a pang of pride for her working class roots; she was the child of a Brooklyn plumber, sitting now with her back straight against the plush red booth, napkin in lap, forearms resting at the table's edge so her elbows were deliberately out of sight. And here was Lucas, who'd grown up in a Connecticut mansion, elbows all over the table, grease-smeared napkin wadded up on his dirty plate, his full mouth ajar. Pauline couldn't bring herself to tell Lucas how bad his manners were. Not to his face—she laughed about it all the time at home.

"Oh, they don't like you, they just don't know how to tell you no," Pauline said. "And, anyway, *why?*" she pressed. "Why eat the same thing every time we come here, twice week?"

Lucas shrugged. "What about you?" he said. "It's not as though you're some adventurous orderer."

"Lucas," Pauline said. She could feel herself becoming unreasonably unnerved, a ripple of hot agitation making its way up her esophagus like acid. This had something to do with how little she respected Lucas, and how upsetting it was to be so attracted to him anyway. "*These are the best pancakes in New York. And anyway, I order a variety. Sometimes I get blueberry, or banana wal-*

nut. These ones have chocolate chips. Jesus Fucking Christ." He laughed, showed another revolting mouthful of his lunch.

This happened sometimes. Pauline was fuming, and Lucas thought she was just being funny.

"Well, this is the best fried-chicken sandwich in New York," he said.

"No," Pauline practically shouted. "That's impossible."

Pauline lived in a detached, three-bedroom house on 21st Avenue in Bensonhurst—where she'd grown up—which she'd inherited when her grandmother died. The house was paid off, but she couldn't afford the taxes; Drew paid all their bills.

Pauline still had a day job, though. She was a dispatcher at her brother-in-law's car service company on 86th Street three or four afternoons a week. It was lousy money, but her sister's husband, Pete, was another excellent source of material. He had over-gelled hair and the thickest Brooklyn accent of anyone Pauline knew. Of course, she had the same accent, but Pete's was much more pronounced—it had not been tamped down by a college education and the self-consciousness that came with fraternizing amongst people who spoke differently. Besides, that slight differentiation was the point of her jokes about him and many other people in her life. When he'd hired her, she'd said, "You know, I went to Fordham. I have a Bachelor's in Philosophy," because it seemed like she should say something about how overqualified she was to work at a cabstand. In general she was overqualified to be living back in Bensonhurst, where the median household income was what two people could earn if one worked full-time as a seamstress and the other at the counter of the pork store, as her grandparents had done, or on the salary of one plumber, especially if that man was in a union like Pauline's father had been.

But still. Pauline wished her sister had reminded Pete about her education, though she knew Marie wasn't all that interested in understanding the fluctuating trajectory of her adulthood. Marie thought Pauline was nuts for taking student loans and then not even bothering to use her degree. Before Pauline moved back to Brooklyn and starting pursuing comedy full-time, Marie had spent a few years worth of holiday gatherings squinting at Pauline as though she were only a loose acquaintance, saying things like, "What's a *sketch comedy troupe*?"

"Yeah, well, you don't need to be a philosopher to do this job," Pete had said, leaning over the sticky desk behind the Plexiglas where they were currently enclosed. The storefront was about the size of a walk-in closet. The white tile was clean, but the place smelled of bleach, stale cigars, and pizza. Pauline was sure she looked tired and old against the fluorescent lights and neon yellow walls.

"The phone rings, pick it up. You press *this* button—" and here Pete jabbed a gray button with his hairy finger. "They say where they're going, when, and you get the *name, address,* write it all down *here*—" and he held up a clipboard with a pencil-marked grid, continued: "And use the radio to tell somebody to take it." He paused, chewed the inside of his cheek. "And look, no disrespect, but try not to be too much of a wiseass."

"What do you mean?" Pauline asked, knowing full well what Pete was getting at.

"You just don't need to make anybody laugh. It's better if you're serious. You know, professional." Then he took the radio's handheld microphone from its helve and began to shout at one of his drivers. "Julio!" he screamed. "Goddamnit, have you picked up Mrs. Ansenelli on Bay Parkway yet?"

It had turned out to be surprisingly difficult job. Pauline had to keep track of the fifteen drivers who were on duty at any given time, and line them up to take the nearest fare once they'd dropped the previous passenger off. Julio was insubordinate and took fares off the street even though it was against the rules. Then Pauline had to deal with the pissed off customers who called to abuse her when he never arrived. If someone wandered into the cabstand looking for a ride, she usually had to lock up and go looking for Mr. Courtly, the seventy-five year old Jamaican man who was on stand-by at the Dunkin Donuts around the corner, where he read the paper all day and flirted with the trapped young girls behind the counter who usually did not pay him any attention. Mr. Courtly claimed that he could neither hear his pager go off, nor could he feel its vibration in his pocket. Half the time he left it in the cab.

Pauline savored the chunk of time when she didn't have to punch in at My Way Ride Service. Her talent agent was getting her good stuff in addition to the bi-weekly gigs at the Laugh Vault, including the highlight of her career so far: three minutes on The Late Show last winter. Sometimes she could get a ride with other comics to play a club in Jersey or Philadelphia. She ultimately wanted television work. Her comedy might start moving forward with greater velocity soon. Besides the TV appearance, last summer she had been listed in a *Time-Out New York* article called "Ten Comediennes To Watch." She'd been interviewed on WNYC, played Ginger's in Chelsea (a very difficult club to book, even on a Wednesday night at eight o'clock), and, every now and then, someone approached her on the subway to say they'd seen her—on Letterman or at some club—and that she was a really funny lady.

Pauline had started sleeping with Lucas shortly after her husband took the job in Kentucky. Like Pauline, Lucas was a comic. Their affair nudged its way into her life from the Laugh Vault—a basement comedy club in Manhattan where Pauline was a regular headliner and Lucas occasionally did ten or fifteen minute openings. Lucas wasn't very funny, but Pauline kind of liked that about him. He was also too young—twenty-five—and not as smart as most of the men she'd been with; he'd gone to Dartmouth and thought that having an Ivy League degree in Film & Media Studies bore witness to his sure intelligence, but it didn't. His education only served as more evidence to what was already obvious: Lucas's family had a lot of money.

Still, there were things about him. For one important thing, he was a big fan of her work. Whenever Pauline had a gig at the Laugh Vault, Lucas hung around the dim light at the club's rear bar. This was the case whether or not Lucas had stage time of his own. (He usually didn't.) But he laughed at Pauline's set, hard, and with what looked like total sincerity, even when her material was old and he'd already heard all the jokes. Sometimes his eyes were still watering when Pauline left the stage and came back to her own greasy leather barstool.

And the affair certainly had its amenities: Lucas's wide-win-dowed Clinton Street apartment, for example—one of those luxury renovations in a grungier part of town, an obvious attempt at a kind of prefabbed coolness that only a wealthy suburbanite would be uncool enough to want. Privately, Pauline thought the place was cheesy, with its reflective wood laminate flooring, track lighting, the stainless steel kitchen that reminded her of an operating room. She thought she could kick a hole through the drywall without hurting herself. But it did have a spacious, superficial extravagance she couldn't help but enjoy. Also, Lucas didn't bother keeping a day job; so long as he lived in a neighborhood like the Lower East Side, his trust fund obfuscated the need for mature ambition, for a plan that might eventually lead to real income. He was always available when Pauline called. She loved waking in the white sheets of Lucas's sun-streaked bedroom. She loved throwing on yesterday's clothes and heading downstairs to yawn over a huge breakfast. She loved watching Lucas pick up the check.

She did not, however, love Lucas. Pauline floated inside the affair as if through a dream—things happened, she enjoyed herself, but when she was alone and unable to keep her thoughts from delving into practicality, Pauline knew her actions weren't without consequence: She was playing at a life that didn't belong to her, acting out a fantasy like a child. Worse, she saw that Lucas really did have feelings for her—he wanted to eventually become a legitimate boyfriend in the wake of the divorce he hoped she'd seek—and she ached to think of her husband, who had no idea how she currently was spending her time. Pauline understood how terribly she was behaving, and her heart raced as she wondered, like the reader of a *Choose Your Own Adventure* Novel, how she'd make it end.

Pauline had met Lucas last November at the Paley Center, where they'd both come to see the cast of *The Ben Stiller Show* reunite as part of the New York Comedy Festival. Drew wouldn't sneak off to interview in Kentucky under the pretense of attending a conference for another two weeks, but, unbeknownst to Pauline at that time, he was in the process of applying for jobs all over the country. He was still working his post-doc job in the biology lab at NYU; out of pity they'd hired him on for an extra semester. He worked all the time, and could rarely get away in time to accompany Pauline to watch or perform comedy. But they always met afterwards, had dinner, and went home together.

After the talk, Lucas walked up and introduced himself. Pauline couldn't decide if he was really so handsome, or if he only appeared that way because his clothing was expensive.

"I've seen you at the Vault a couple times," he said. "You're really funny."

"Oh!" she said. "Thank you. That's so nice."

But the conversation flew over the horizon when Lucas said

"I'm opening there next Wednesday. My first real gig." His smile was either sheepish or an excellent imitation of sheepishness. Pauline nodded. "A comic in a Burberry jacket," she said. "That is... unprecedented."

Lucas laughed. Pauline was having a hard time resisting the urge to do crowd work. Of course, off-stage, crowd work was just flirting.

"Well, good luck to you," she said. "If I were in the audience, I'm sure I'd want to laugh at you, but people tend to favor an unfortunate looking comic. You're too attractive, and even if you were ugly enough, you can't go around telling jokes in designer clothes." She wanted to go on about designer clothes, what made them unpalatable to club audiences, who were a generally dorky bunch. He could do well with the Midwestern college girls who came to New York for internships at places like MTV and Condé Nast. They only liked the surface of the jokes, anyway. There was a bit in here, Pauline felt close to cracking into the crunchy joke nut that hid beneath every conversation's lumpy shell.

Lucas raised his eyebrows. "You say that as though you're unattractive."

"Oh, I'm smoking hot for a comic," Pauline smiled, sure to show her crooked bottom teeth, which were small and unnoticeable.

If Drew were there, he'd have leaned over and whispered, *You're on*, which meant she should turn it *off*—stop performing in casual conversation. She had a tendency to get away from herself. Things were fine when she wasn't standing; Pauline had no ability to be a comic while sitting down, but milling about—at parties, on long lines, in auditoriums like this one—she got nervous and revved into action.

She didn't yet know how old Lucas was; he could be twenty-two or thirty. Most of the aspiring comics she met after shows and at events like this were quite young. College kids whose view did not yet hold the gray carpet of waiting rooms for sitcom and soda commercial auditions, the countless nights of being bumped from a gig when someone funnier or better-known rolled into a club looking to work out new material, the lunches with suited network bozos who'd finally just come out with it and admit they were looking, really, for an *actor*, someone who could *play* funny but wasn't limited to anecdotal pantomime. Pauline would never have pursued comedy if she hadn't had Drew to support her, financially and otherwise. And now she was standing in this auditorium with a comic who looked like a model. And Drew—her husky, good-natured scientist—had only just gotten off work and was no-doubt waiting outside the 8th Avenue Shake Shack in the rain, in the cheap windbreaker he'd bought at Marshall's. Pauline was already a few minutes late; she needed to get to him. But for reasons she could not quite understand, she first needed to touch the quilted fabric of Lucas's jacket collar. He showed no surprise when she reached up and gently massaged his coat between her thumb and finger. It was even softer than she'd imagined. "I've gotta run," she said, letting go slowly. "My husband's waiting."

"You're married," Lucas said, not well concealing his disappointment. "You don't wear a wedding ring."

"No," she said, looking down at her pale, chapped hands. "I don't."

Drew's work was going to be featured in *Pest Control Technology* magazine.

"That's not an actual publication," Pauline said when he called to tell her about it. But it was. It was a *trade* magazine, not something you found at the supermarket next to *People* and *Redbook*. This meant that businesses—not universities or research foundations—might read about him; maybe he could get into the private sector.

"If I could get a job as a manufacturing consultant," he said, "I could make a lot of money working with design engineers to invent some synthetic mattress cover that mimics what the kidney bean leaf does—"

Pauline interrupted: "Wouldn't that be uncomfortable?"

"Trichomes are microscopic," Drew said. His words were clipped in a way that only Pauline could detect and perceive as annoyance. He'd said all this before, to Pauline—many times—about the trichomes, about the kidney bean leaf's razor-like hairs being bed bug-sized, soft seeming to a human's comparatively gigantic touch. This was not extra information on the topic of Drew's work: It was the information itself. Pauline knew this, she did, but her mind had buried the practicalities of her husband's job beneath its more amusing implications. Without being reminded, she could only recall the old Estonian woman who was a product of her own imagination.

"I'm sorry," Pauline said, and she was. "I don't even know why I asked that."

"The point," Drew said, "Is that if I could get a job like that, I could come back to New York. No more following measly grants to places like Lexington."

"How is it there right now?" Pauline asked. "Is it warm?"

"It's about seventy. Sunny," Drew said. "How's Brooklyn?"

"Rainy and cold, and, as usual, reeking of Chinese food and wet garbage," Pauline said.

"I really miss you," Drew said.

"I miss you, too."

"I don't think we should split up."

This was the way about every third phone call went. Drew had good news about his career, Pauline congratulated him, or meant to offer congratulations before they slipped down into the thick familiarity of their marriage, into the soft, sweet muck of their having known and loved each other for the better part of a decade. Pauline's affair came into sharp focus, revealing its shameful yellow twinge. She thought of leaving New York on the next flight out to Kentucky. She'd make the kind of sacrifices wives made for their hard-working, understanding men, drive a Toyota Highlander to Target, get her hair cut at the only Aveda salon in town. She would buy a Vera Bradley handbag—the bizarre paisley duffel that was common, alongside pink manicures and pastel embroidered denim, on the tourist ladies who sometimes came to the comedy club—and a large dog. Maybe a St. Bernard. She would, eventually, begin to convincingly pronounce words like *y'all*.

The problem, then, was the other two-thirds of their conversations, which were pocked by the holes of their very different lives. Drew was still a scientist and Pauline was still rooted to show business, to New York, and her cheating with Lucas was still the angry punishment she was inflicting upon their future.

But now all she said to Drew was, "So let's not split up, then."

"We need to plan everything around each other," Drew said. "Not just say 'someday we'll have the things we want and then we'll be a normal couple.' Because it's always going to be about someday."

But the thing about the house was that she couldn't give it up. It was something that couldn't move away from her, couldn't expect anything from her, and—now that her mother was in Florida and her dad and Nonna and Grandad were all dead, and Marie and Pete had that gaudy place in Dyker Heights—the house was what was left of who Pauline had been before she'd had to make any decisions about what kind of woman she was supposed to become. In the house, she felt like a kid, safe from whatever she might want her own funniness to mean in the scheme of her adulthood. And, anyway, when Pauline thought of driving a Highlander around a southern state's suburbs, she wasn't really picturing herself. She was imagining a woman who could do things she couldn't do. She was imagining, for example, a woman with a driver's license.

Lucas was up that evening, doing his best bit. It was about romantic hot-air balloon rides. Under the pulsating yellow lights on the small triangular stage, he explained with just the right amount of indignation that hot-air balloons were the antithesis of a romantic vehicle—they were technologically antiquated flying machines, and therefore terrifying. He did a decent sound effect of the propane burner that, coupled with the wind, apparently made in-flight conversation impossible on a hot-air balloon.

From the bar, Pauline turned to watch. She'd seen this set a couple dozen times already. The audience always laughed. Not hard, people weren't bending their heads down to their tables or wiping tears away, but it was solid. It made Pauline smile. But she also thought: *So?* It was such an obvious abstraction: *Of course* hot-air balloons were only an ideal of romance. *Romance itself was only an ideal.* This was the fundamental difference between the kind of hostile, "smarty-pants-in-a-dumb-world" comedy Lucas and so many younger men favored—the kind of comedy that was most popular on the college circuit and with the YouTube clip watchers—and the comedy Pauline made. Lucas's sets were self-referential but insincere and impersonal. True, he had been in a hot-air balloon, but only with his parents while on vacation in Saint-Tropez.

Pauline knew that her burgeoning success was due, in part, to an appearance of effortlessness, to the comfortable space her body took up on stage and the conversational quality of her delivery. It wasn't easy. This was something that had taken years to get a handle on; Pauline had done her first open-mic when she was a nineteen year old college sophomore; no one had laughed. She had long forgotten the content of those early attempts, but the content was only half relevant in any case. She hadn't been able to sound unaffected on stage for years. She hadn't known how to turn mere funniness into comedy; the two were so different.

Of course, content mattered somewhat. Pauline didn't set herself up as someone who saw what was wrong with the world the way Lucas did; she gave her audience credit enough to recognize that the world was a silly place without her insistence. So she joked about her shit job, about her heavily accented, ravioli eating family, about her selfishness in refusing to move away with her husband. "I just don't think I can get the kind of rejection I'm looking for anywhere else," she explained in one bit. She had a willingness to inhabit the whole joke, and not merely be a jester: Pauline's jokes about her husband told the story of failing marriage. She didn't have to come out and say this. If she had, it would have ceased to be funny. The humor was not in what was obvious or overarching: Bed bugs weren't really funny. They'd ruin your furniture and bite your face. Pauline's jokes about Pete and her sister—their hair, their accents, their clothes—were really about her loneliness in being the one who'd changed. Her material didn't outright address how close she'd been to Marie, or that the sound of the elevated train rumbling a few blocks from her grandparents house made her think, every time she heard it, of her dish-gloved mother, widowed and chain smoking in front of the television in Ft. Lauderdale. Pauline missed her fiercely. And she missed her father, her grandparents, hated the sound of her lone feet hitting the carpeted steps in their house. Her joke about that horrible sea-foam shag carpet gave her a chance, for a few minutes on the stage, to feel good about being in that house all alone. To laugh about Drew not being in the kitchen, telling the Mr. Face to get off the table. These jokes provided the kind of release that only came with hard work.

"A hot-air balloon," Lucas was saying, his complexion not even a little shiny from the stage's incubator heat, the armpits of his blue Armani polo shirt uncannily dry, "looks so tranquil in the poster they hang on the ceiling above my dentist's chair." The audience laughed. That detail about the dentist's chair had been Pauline's; she'd given it to him, as a gift. "But it's not so serene once you're up there and you realize: 'This is a life threatening situation'." Lucas's inflection was such an obvious imitation of Jerry Seinfeld that sometimes Pauline couldn't stand it.

Not that she didn't appreciate Seinfeld's tame observational cynicism, or even Lucas's application of it. But a good comic would start out imitating, eventually developing those forgeries into something less wooden than what Lucas was enacting just then. Lucas wasn't a comic; he was a handsome man—far too attractive and young to be parroting Seinfeld, for god sakes—who happened to be funny and who liked attention. And lucky Lucas: Crowds loved men. When a male comic came onto the stage, the energy in the room was just what it should be. Everyone thought, *Let's see what this guy is about*. About one in every ten performers was a woman, and Pauline was the only woman recognized as a regular, as one of the club's draw-ins. When women took the stage, the club's energy shifted to skepticism. The sense was—even among the half of the audience who happened to be women themselves—*This isn't going to be as good. This is* lady *comedy*.

To a certain extent, Pauline understood. So many of the women she worked alongside performed unadventurous diet-and-shopping sets that were unconsciously and sickeningly sexist. Pauline knew a comic named Lindsay Gelbert whose sets focused entirely on her desire to get married—she even had a little prop veil. She spoke in a baby voice. But what bothered Pauline was how Lindsay couldn't just be a shitty comic, she had to be the definition of female comedy itself—why? Her shtick wasn't worse than half of Lucas's lame jokes about stupid fucking hot-air balloons.

When Lucas's set was done, he hurried over to her. Pauline smiled, took a long swallow of beer.

"How was that?" he asked.

"That was great."

"Yeah," he said. "I was really on tonight, you know? I feel like they laugh a little harder every time."

"That's how it works," Pauline said. She gestured to the bartender for another drink.

Pauline had an audition for a cough syrup commercial. It was a principal spot on a national run, which meant thousands and thousands of dollars in residuals. It could air for a year or more. On primetime, probably. She was reading for the part of a twenty-something woman sick with a cold, tossing and turning in a tank top and pair of pajama shorts, described in the script as CUTE, YOUNG—NOT TOO SEXY, until, unable to stand the discomfort and exhaustion any longer, she gets out of bed and goes sneezing and hacking into a dim-lit apartment kitchen. There, her chic but bespeckled roommate (wearing silk button down PROFESSIONAL LOOKING pajamas) sits at the table in front of a laptop, presumably working late into the night, as young professionals in the city are wont to do, and advises the sickly role Pauline was after that the leading brand cold medicine would leave her groggy in the morning. However, the patented formula in Flunot™ would ease her symptoms, induce sleep, and have her feeling energized for her big interview tomorrow morning. Pauline was going to say, "So Flunot™ takes care of everything?" to which her mature, business savvy roommate would reply, "Except acing your interview. That's all you," and then give a reassuring smile.

It wasn't comedy. Not purposefully, at least. It was an

insulting attempt to market a hypnotic acetaminophen cocktail to young women who were sick all the time because they worked and drank and wanted too much in filthy cities. Pauline looked young, still got ID'ed at the bar more than half the time, and would lie at her audition, claim to be twenty-six.

The commercial was stupid and embarrassing, but if she got it she could quit the cabstand and get a learner's permit—again—and try—again—for a driver's license, buy a car. She wanted the well-paying state college gigs, and the exposure that came with going on the road. She ultimately wanted to write a television show about a Brooklyn comic married to a scientist. But, unless she got something like this lame commercial, the only way she could currently afford to do that was to sell her grandparents' house and move to Lexington. She'd Googled "Comedy clubs in Kentucky." There were three. She'd like to play them, sure. But afterwards she'd like to head home, stopping in a couple other three-venue states along the way.

The morning of the audition, Pauline was eating cornflakes over the kitchen sink when her stomach lurched with a sudden strong nausea and her mind made the startling move away from her ambitions: She realized with slick terror that she did not know how long it had been since she'd had her last period. At the large wall calendar above the kitchen table where her cat was currently sleeping, she counted backwards from May into April. Upstairs, in her bedroom, she snapped the plastic birth control case open and tried to make sense of the amount of pills therein. There were nine. What did that mean? In what she had begun to think of as her real life, Drew had reminded her each morning to take her pill. If he left for work before she woke, he brought the case to the night stand with a glass of water and a large note, something along the lines of: PAULINE TAKE THESE PLEASE XOXO.

Pauline had been to Rite Aid and back when Lucas called, and had a neat row of three positive pregnancy tests. In the doorway of her pink and black checkered bathroom, she was sure she was not herself. She couldn't be the producer of those six blue lines, displayed in perfect lucidity along the sink's ledge. She wasn't the woman, swallowing hard until the tight sob creeping up her throat receded back into her stomach, who was hitting the answer button on her iPhone, saying, "Yeah, hey."

But she was, and from the lilt in his voice, Lucas's life had also shifted out of frame sometime in the thirty-six hours since they'd last spoken.

Lucas said, "Are you home? I'm headed down there now."

"What?" Pauline asked. "Down where?"

"To Brooklyn. Listen, what's your address?"

She was waiting on the stoop when Lucas pulled up in the silver Lexus he sometimes borrowed from a college friend. Lucas had never been to Pauline's house. If he came to Brooklyn at all, it was to bars and venues in the hip, gentrifying northern neighborhoods.

"I never realized how far out you live," Lucas said, surveying the street's paved lawns and short brick townhouses, the aluminum awnings and Italian flags and ceramic St. Anthony shrines. He looked now at the house's vinyl facade and Pauline could not read his reaction. Maybe her assumption of his supercilious politesse kept her from gauging his true opinion. He knew enough about Bensonhurst from her comedy, sure, but she felt protective of it now. "Your house is bigger than I'd imagined." Pauline just stared at him.

When he realized that he wasn't going to be invited in, Lucas asked if Pauline wanted to go for coffee. There was a place, she said, a few minutes away. In Bay Ridge.

Inside the Lexus, Lucas said, "So how're you?"

"I have that commercial audition at 3:30," Pauline said.

"Why are you here?"

"Right. I have some news." There was a pressured pause. "I need to talk to you, actually." They drove under the elevated tracks, and the passing train made it impossible to say anything for a while. Lucas was clearly rattled by the awesome noise and energy the raised subway made.

"Here," Pauline said. "Just park here—it's only a block."

The café was not really a café. Rather, Pauline had brought Lucas to the Societa San Calogero: a meeting place for Italians—mostly old men—to play Scopa and watch soccer games that came through the massive satellite dish affixed to the fire escape. She loved it here. Maybe she liked the Society Hall, as it was known in the neighborhood, better than any place in Manhattan, or anywhere else in the world. She'd never written a joke about it, though she'd thought of a few.

The interior was a hodgepodge of card tables in the center and restaurant booths lining the walls, which were decorated with cheap paintings of the saints and popes and some faded posters of the 1982 World Cup. The room smelled of strong coffee, aftershave, and cigars. It smelled like Pauline's grandpa. Pauline had brought Lucas here out of some defensive instinct. It seemed important to communicate to him that she had an identity a wealthy person couldn't buy, to demonstrate the ways in which her life was interesting *because* she was not rich. Pauline had the sense that Lucas didn't see how she really was this person, not just someone who joked like it was pretend. So she spoke to John at the counter in the sifted Italian she used with old people, and was sure Lucas noticed that she wasn't charged for their espresso.

"So," Lucas said the minute they sat down outside where there were two tables with wicker cafe chairs and a view of the Verrazano. "Remember the part I got in that web series a while ago?" Pauline nodded. "It never happened," she said, as if reminding Lucas of this fact.

"Yeah, well, Ryan Keene, the writer/producer guy?"

"Yes, I know him," Pauline tried not to sound impatient. *But get on with it*, she was thinking. And so he did. Ryan Keene had spent the last couple months shopping the proposed web series, called *Broseph and Joey*, to cable networks. And it had only taken a few meetings before it was picked up for a pilot. And Lucas, who played Joey, was going to L.A. to start shooting in three weeks.

"Just like that," Pauline said. Her face felt heavy from the strain of trying to hold up a mild expression.

"Just like that," Lucas said, breathless, finally sweating for once in his life.

Pauline realized now that Lucas had always had a better shot at getting what Pauline so badly wanted, despite how much funnier they both knew she was, and how much longer she'd been working—his looks, his charm, his being a man—and becoming famous or something close to famous. She managed to congratulate him, but her thoughts were petty. Few pilots ever made it onto the air.

"The other thing," Lucas said, his voice going apologetic, "is that I've been thinking. About you being married."

"Oh have you." Pauline didn't intone a question.

"You're not getting a divorce?" Now Lucas was making a statement that sounded like a question. Pauline looked down the street, toward the bridge. In high school, her history teacher had told the class that Robert Moses once described the Verrazano-Narrows as "a triumph of simplicity and restraint over exuberance." She'd forgotten that until just this moment.

Lucas was still talking: "...and with me going to California, and getting the TV show—"

"You got a *pilot*," Pauline said, returning her attention to him. She didn't care that she sounded wounded and jealous; Lucas was about to make it very awkward for her to ask him for money and a ride to Planned Parenthood.

"Right, a pilot," Lucas conceded. "Still. I like you, but we aren't dating, right? You're married, so that says to me that we aren't dating, and if the show *is* ordered—"

Pauline held up her hand. "You can stop," she said. "I get it. And it's obviously okay. I'm willing to bet you'll end up staying out in L.A., anyway."

"And you aren't leaving your husband," Lucas said. "Admit it. Say it."

"Why?" Pauline was shaky from caffeine and her own pregnant nerves. "Things are more complicated for me than they are for you."

"That's your own fault," Lucas said.

"Not necessarily."

"Okay, fine, Pauline. But I don't know why you won't just say it. You aren't going to leave your husband. You don't want to be with me. You could at least admit that."

It was all true, but she couldn't. She could only say, "I have to get ready for my audition." Lucas looked exasperated to the point of tears. Pauline could not bear to think what pathetic thing he might say if she divulged what she'd been doing when he called. So they went off in a silence that was too thick to cut through, even to say a proper goodbye when the Lexus pulled back onto 21st Avenue.

Pauline played the Laugh Vault two days later. Lucas wasn't there. She hadn't expected him, of course. After saying hello and thank-you, she asked the audience, "Who here is from New York?" Besides the first two rows, she couldn't see the crowd through the lights, but it sounded as though more than half clapped and hooted. "No," she said. "Who's *from* New York? I don't give a shit if you moved here for college." The club was on Thompson Street, surrounded by NYU's ever expanding empire. There were titters, but no more applause. Pauline knew she was being uncharacteristically aggressive toward the crowd. Like a man. She softened, shrugged. "Because, see, I'm from Brooklyn, and I'm starting to think I'm going to die there, too."

This was new material, but Pauline was finding that, like old, hard memorized bits, she didn't need to concentrate much. This could mean it just wasn't very good. The set focused on life in New York, on how everyone wanted to be here, and everyone here hated it but couldn't leave, couldn't imagine any place better.

Pauline said, "New York makes you nuts. Thomas Wolfe said—" here she interrupted herself to add, "And I'm up here quoting Tom Wolfe because I'm definitely not an asshole." She paused for the laughter. "He said, basically, that a person becomes a New Yorker within five minutes. And that's gotta be true, because it takes about five minutes of being in the city before you go crazy. And New York is just the world's biggest insane asylum." She went into an anecdote about an argument she'd had with Pete on the way to Atlantic Terminal once, and as she told it, she found herself squinting past the bar, toward the door. She had a sense that, magically, Drew might appear now that Lucas was gone. That he'd know she needed him to see this and tell her it was funny.

But Drew was in Kentucky. The thought of his distance was a hard lump in her throat. That soreness was enclosed in what she was going to do—ask her sister for money for an abortion? Spend Drew's money, and then lie and say it had been for something else? She didn't think she could do either. Nor could she even wrap her mind around the inevitable infant that would result from inaction. Thinking all this, Pauline was sure she'd lose her voice in the middle of her time. She worried also that her jangling hormones could send her into a tearful fit, right there under the lights.

But Pauline didn't lose her voice. Or cry. She finished her bit without forgetting the jokes, and then, after attaching the microphone back to its stand with a steady grip, she descended back into the crowd.

NAOMI MULVIHILL

INVITATION

A mallard bathes in meltwater at the pond's southern curve, his cautionary
orange feet, practical and rubbery as galoshes.

Beneath the pitted mother-of-pearl there must be a still place
waiting —under a latch-hole, a hundred kinds of blackness

and a flowering, somewhere, of gills. Tread lightly,
the mallard says, leaving a faint herringbone of prints in the snow.

My friend —a student of Buber, who fills her sideboard with receipts
and paper roses and a peach that's shrunk away from its skin—

says she's not eating much these days by which she means everything
she does not eat helps her grow empty enough

to receive the world. I'm confused by violence against the self
in service of the spiritual, though I'm

given to violence myself. Exit the elevator at level 4
where patients wear regular clothes

and no window opens. In the ward's café, a woman named Roxanne
hatches her wedding plans. The whiskered attendant

will be maid of honor. Come. Everyone will be there. Mauve tabletops
conceal their bolted pedestals. A man paces inside

a set of eight linoleum squares. When my friend speaks to me
of an agony of narrowness I don't know

how to listen. I think instead of an animated film I've seen, every picture
made in sand, of a skater who as she turned became a fissure in the ice, into which

she vanished.

DENMARK:
Variations 1, 2, 5

Version of Hamlet in which the ghost never reappears. The first three scenes occur as in the original. In act I scene 4 Hamlet, Horatio, and Marcellus enter and deliver their lines as written, up to Hamlet's speech ("it is a custom/more honor'd in the breach, than the observance" etc). After which the three actors remain onstage, waiting, expectant, until the last member of the audience leaves; at which point the actors may do as they wish.

Version of Hamlet in which every character who has lost a father continually howls. This includes not only Hamlet, Fortinbras, and later Ophelia and Laertes; but, additionally, Polonius, Claudius, Gertrude, and the ghost itself. Some scenes become a gathering of characters howling; others are a strange mixture of certain characters howling while the rest struggle to be heard.

Version of Hamlet in which the prince never appears. All other characters speak their lines as indicated in the script. When it is time for Hamlet to speak, there is silence. It is clear that the other characters know something is missing; there is the sense of mourning in the air. Horatio, in particular, seems unable to meet the others' eyes.

THE WOODS

When I hear the bell, I come forth, an ataxic rook in heels.
Yes, it's true that I multiply like a queen, but my needle

betrays me, unconvinced. Hit the switch when I audition my dance
and bare my neck. In the ice storm scene

I peacock into a spiral sequence and lose my skate blade. Oh dear,
I left my dream girl in the woods. Don't be pissed

when my hot air balloon gets tangled in your tree.
I'd rather basket berries than take your fallacies apart

in my coroner sombrero. Women teeter in bird of paradise pose
and I flatten into origami that's not your ornament

or secret valentine. It's twisted how I make lines, branch
over branch. The maps recalculate as I call *do over*

and stumble off with the decoy.

The Guru

The Guru was once a baby boy, and He was born to worldly parents.

At least His mother was present; His father had walked off in the most profane manner. The baby boy was full of the knowledge of human suffering. His mother was an old gray horse at twenty-six, and His father's curses were drowned out on the factory floor in a different city.

His fresh baby tissue was made of old human letters. Bleary lead, clogged ink, brittle paper.

There was no star over His cot, no herbal fug of cow breath moistening His blankets. Stars were brass and valor in Soviet Russia, stars were because there were so few streetlamps. Cows were starved and slaughtered. Why weren't they slaughtered before they starved? the baby boy already wondered.

But He wasn't to be an expert on world hunger.

There were no nurses in the provincial hospital. (His mother had traveled south to her mother to have Him.) Only shuffling babushkas who quit chewing their lips to stare at Him.

But the baby boy wasn't born to save the class of kerchiefs, He wasn't born to light dead streetlamps. The baby boy had the knowledge of a billion stars already. He knew a billion souls of suffering.

Hospitals then you brought your own soap and your own towel. You brought the chicken leg in a jar of broth. Do you hear Me? said the Guru.

You squit to shit—squot? said the Guru—the walls of the shitter like falling down a well.

Do you hear Me? Nobody told you when you were finished giving birth. Not the babushkas. The trees outside were black spires.

My own mother hoped to die, said the Guru. Even so, My baby urine did not trickle but splashed like a baptismal fountain.

Lay your subhuman at My feet, people, said the Guru. My feet are just feet, formed from a baby's pudding. The little bobs and yellow crystals. My feet can take it, people.

There was a lot of weeping. A lot of laughter after sorrow.

A boy from the baby. It was clear He was different. When they went to the "uncle's" dacha in summer, the boy dreamed the figs on the platter. Cucumbers came to be as a result of His dreaming. His body was golden in the farm pond. The drunkard farmer saw an angel and quit drinking. There were a thousand other drunkard farmers, pensioners, everybody, but the boy did not want to attract attention. He already had with His gift for piano. The uncle was all accordion and bluster.

When the boy was nineteen He went to Altai in the Himalayas. He went to Kyoto.

At some point He showed up in Berkeley, California.

Then He made His hermitage-sanctuary in the shell of an old farm behind the Atlantic.

We found Him where He had built His lair against that dour seascape.

Plenty of people had come before us.

Devotion was free. Practice would cost you everything.

An aromatic deck made a fan around the low waist of the zendo. We sat on the soft cedar skirt, we learned how He had curled His hand inside His mother's and transmitted the Great Happiness of His being.

His wives wept long gray tears when they told us. Dark eyes were gopi-girl, were Hindu goddess. If we closed our eyes we could see into the kohl-dark corners of temples slicked with clay-tasting waters, the crown of a red tower redder than sunset, and the pale hairs rose, pulling the flesh of our forearms into tiny starpoints.

DEREK JG WILLIAMS

NOT BLOOD

Features of the moon: the craters your fists
    punched-out, spider-webbed plaster,

milky white bruises—your vacant blue eyes
        as I dragged the heavy chains of you
           from our house.

I lived beside you like a prisoner
    after you returned, carrying your chains

as best I could. I wasn't yet prepared for living
        and you were too young to leave
           for good.

Brother, you need more than can be given.
    I learned your rules the hard way

back when I was only trying to make it long
        enough to move out
           and move on.

But I never did find you after that day.
    I carry its weight wherever I go—

our house in aftermath, silent as the moon's
        dead oceans where waves
           once shone.

We're not blood, and the snake of not blood
    coils behind your teeth, waiting

to be unleashed—we're brothers, craters
        filled with teeth, bound
           by a word.

JACOB SUNDERLIN

[I HAVE SKIMMED OVER THE WORLD IN THIS GREEN CANOE]

I have skimmed over the world on this green canoe
like a water bug, Hank Williams. There is nothing
more solitary than the green canoe at midnight,
squirrely & drunk with one of you weird believers.
We wear a thing called a forehead—it is a lamp, a
third eye, illuminating the silent arc of the toothy
unconverted. Were you a fishing man, Hank Williams,
or a walleye? Were you lured from some crater, or
were you clustered in canoes against an ordinary
night, leaning in close, imagining the bats that
swooped out over the water & between our heads
were ordinary bats.

[OH, HANK WILLIAMS, HOW BOOTLEG YOU IS. WHEN YOU]

Oh, Hank Williams, how bootleg you is. When you
leave, you never really leave—you just thread
another page off the book & stare through the
wobble of mason jars to find me there, wearing
camouflage. I'm taking off my worldview with a
knife. I get this hovel idea sometimes—it's filled
with pelts, an old woodstove, a clawfoot wash tub
in a cabin built of necessary trees. You're always
there, making the most of some hermitage, filling
buckets with the milk of cheese-making goats who
have biblical names, like Jacob, like Budweiser.

ELEGY IN WHICH A BIRD APPEARS

I will make of my mind a scrape nest for your absence. Clear a swale
for silences. Hollow it deep. Let it wild be with sorrow.
Let it small psalm home again. And when it becomes difficult
to imagine nothing as solid as a mother's arms, I will keep on moving
through the grasses in search of smallness, seeds & husks blowing
in the paper air of your voice as I remember it—a quiet abyss.
For this parting takes muscle unnatural. Lift me
into the sun again. I hardly have hands to touch
my sutures. Even the clouds coldly sway. My wrists—
pale fish—move through the surfaces of winter ponds.
Edges, I hover. Every hill becomes a ruin.
Beneath my nails—dredged earth of heaven, black moon-slivers
in shades of hair. And I wonder, in this un-day of your leaving, why all
you send me is a bird? Hungry, wing-fluttered, jawing for a song.

DEVON TAYLOR

THERE IS A LIFE

It all came apart so slowly. Every part was a necessary step in the dismantling. Even the first step, the day fifteen years before when Mom and Dad drove past the farm, sprawled out over acres grown wild with disuse. It was just months into their marriage and they were still drunk on the possibility of fresh starts and love that lasts forever—the evidence of their past mistakes asleep in the back seat, the evidence of their future ones asleep in her womb. They pulled to the side of Buddtown Road, stepped out of the car, the weeds high around their calves, and saw the 'For Sale' sign. That was the first pull in the fabric.

But how could they know? A new love begs to be challenged, to prove that it's invincible. Go ahead, pour your money into this farm, your sweat and your hours. Peel paper off the walls of that old ruined farmhouse and hammer down nails in the floorboards. Fill these pastures with horses that need bales of hay and new shoes every month and expensive bridles and saddles.

I'll pay the bills, you build this farm, my Dad might have said. And he would have meant it, would have loved the idea of Mom, her long blond hair pulled back in a pony tail, painting kitchen cabinets and hanging buckets in the barn. He in a suit, she in a pair of jeans. Mom was two years removed from a job teaching English to seventh graders, a job she despised, that she fled, along with her ex-husband. She'd spent a year hot-walking horses on the racetrack and teaching riding lessons at a local stable. As a lawyer, Dad made enough money to feel like it was a lot of money—*enough money for both of us*, he might have said. Go ahead, their love pushed, buy this farm.

And in those golden 1980s, the first decade of my childhood, it worked. She laid tile and he wrote legal briefs and they went to Friday night auctions and bought horses and ponies. They bred the mares and stayed up late when they foaled. They plunked riding helmets on the heads of my sisters, my brother, and me. She taught us to push our heels down in the stirrups when we rode, and he offered clueless, kind words like *You look good up there* or *Our own little National Velvet*. And they marveled at what they had created.

Our days were not stagnant, but marked with constant reminders of *life*. Foals born, ponies that bucked and galloped across the fields, mutts that trotted onto the farm and stayed, and litters upon litters of kittens. I was the lone product of both of my parents, my older brother and sisters from each of their first failed attempts. And in the way of the youngest, life had a permanence to it. I could look at everyone older than me and feel like the track never strayed far from the familiar. Life moved, but each day the movement felt simple and predictable. *Dresden had a filly last night* or *We better get the horses in before it storms*. It was safe and never-ending.

It's easy to look back now and see the cracks. In lieu of a business model, my parents opted for *we'll figure it out later*. They grew attached to horses they needed to sell, to horses' owners that got behind on board. Dad's nightly gin-and-tonic ritual stopped having the charm of those first couple of years where everything is funny, where everything is foreplay, where even the boozy, uncoordinated groping of one-too-many is sexy. And Mom's dreams grew beyond the four corners of our South Jersey farm to show circuits in Florida and Vermont, to the chance for us kids to *really compete*. Maybe it felt to him like she was seeing past him, past their life and marriage. And when she returned with us after a weekend away at a show and found him slumped at the kitchen table, drowning his sixth, perhaps it felt to her like there was no absence in her departure and no thrill in her return.

These things can go on for years. There's comfort in anything if it becomes routine. I was a young girl then and the halcyon days of that first decade bled into my teenage years when I woke at night to my parents fighting downstairs and tiptoed through mornings when their stony silence filled the room. Over time, it, too, became simple and predictable.

If it wasn't the drinking or the horses, it was the money that ultimately did them in. By the time I was fourteen, my parents were two mortgages deep and living on credit cards. There were *too many* horses, *too many* acres, *too many* dreams. My sisters were all grown and gone by then, my brother soon to follow. The farm stopped being a vehicle for my parents' love, stopped being a place they could raise children and paint cabinets and grow together.

Cheryl was just an excuse for my Dad, a way out. Her kids took riding lessons and she was going through a rough patch with her husband—she approached Dad for legal advice and it wasn't long before the affair started. Maybe he looked at her, a part-time cleaning lady, part-time bus driver, and saw someone who might not have dreams too big for him. But it didn't matter what he saw; what mattered was what he didn't, which was a life with us, with me, with Mom, with the farm. He moved across town with Cheryl two months shy of my fifteenth birthday.

Mom kept it up for a bit—tried to make a go at keeping the business, the horses, and the boarders. Maybe she realized it wasn't the same without him there, without even the idea of him there—Dad who hadn't set foot in the barn in months, if not years. Or maybe she just ran out of steam. The farm never gave back as much as it promised. After a few months she took up with a new boyfriend: a soft, kind electrician named Milt who lived a couple of miles away. A month after my fifteenth birthday, they were engaged. She quit teaching riding lessons and sold off almost everything—horses, equipment, the trailer. The horses that were left were a couple of ponies, a school horse, Elsa, an old broodmare, Dresden, and a handful of self-sufficient boarders.

Elsa and Dresden had lived in the back pasture for years. In her heyday broodmare years, Dresden was a gorgeous, albeit high-strung Thoroughbred with a rich, dark coat and ears that twitched. Elsa spent the better part of her years teaching little kids to ride. She was a wide, flat-backed Quarter Horse who embodied slow-and-steady—the mini-van to Dresden's sports car. By the time they reached old age, Dresden's sight was going, causing her even more anxiety, and Elsa was a cranky old bat. Set out to pasture together, the two were an unlikely pair, but they took to one another like a couple of widowed old ladies with no one else left in the world. In the back field, they ambled across the acres, or stood side by side with their noses stuck in the grass. In the hot summer months when the black flies swarmed, they would stand next to one another, facing in opposite directions, and swish flies off each other's faces. After most of the horses were sold and the barn was empty, it made sense to bring them inside and give them their own stalls. But it was like separating a foal from her mother. Even in neighboring stalls, they neighed for one another and paced back and forth frantically. After a couple of days, we gave up and let them loose in the pasture again where they resumed their afternoon walks.

During the summer, when Dad was gone and Mom was off falling in love and who knows where my brother was, I moved through the barn and along the fence railings with the air of an empty-nester. The quiet never lost its pitch, never grew to feel simple and predictable. But if I perched on a post along the back field and watched Elsa and Dresden deep in a patch of summer clover, I could almost grasp that long-forgotten sense of permanence. With my back to the barn and the acres of empty pastures, I could imagine them full, that the barn hummed with the whoosh of hay pitched, the pounding of a blacksmith's hammer, the clip of a cross-tie, the voices of pony kids and reluctant parents and the easy cadence of my mother at the center of it all.

No one else was there when Dresden hemorrhaged. I don't recall many of the details—just that it was early on a July evening, an hour or two of light left in the day, and I was the only one home. I remember my mother was away that weekend, though I don't know where, or why. I don't know if I heard Dresden's cries of distress or if I was filling up the water trough and saw it all happen. I do know that by the time Dr. Hanson arrived, the sun was all but gone, and he said there was nothing he could do, nothing that anyone could have done. *Severe renal hemorrhage. That's a death sentence.* Two images stay lodged in my memory: Dresden, all at once panicked and resigned to *needing us*, to *needing something*, eye-balling us as she stood clipped to the end of a lead shank, her coat dark in the gloaming; and, after her body had been hauled away and Dr. Hanson was gone, leading Elsa into the barn, her hooves heavy on the concrete, the sway of her back, and the slope of her neck, and thinking *It's just you now, Elsa.*

The next morning one of the boarders was there when I strolled into the barn. Lynn, a pretty middle-aged woman with a tiny frame who fancied herself something of a cowgirl, who rented out several stalls in the barn and eked out an existence buying and selling thoroughbreds off the track. She took care of our last remaining horses in exchange for a little break in the board. I'd left a note filling her in on the details the night before. *She okay?* I asked when I saw Lynn. *Fine. Ate her breakfast like nothing.* Good old Elsa. Solid as a truck.

By noon Elsa was stamping at the sawdust and turning to peer at her side, a distinct rumble in the barrel of her belly. Even at fifteen, I knew colic. Horses have delicate, complex digestive systems. It doesn't take much—too much water, a shift in diet, a stressful trailer ride—to send their abdomens into spasm or, worse, put a kink or block in their intestines. Something like ten percent of horses colic at one point or another and, though it can be fatal, it can also be merely a minor hiccup in a horse's morning. I'd stood with Mom and looked over the top of a stall door to a horse inside pawing at the ground and nipping at his side. *You have to get them out of their stalls and hold them,* Mom used to tell me, *because if they roll on the ground, they can twist their intestines and rupture them. They'll be dead within minutes.*

I slid a halter over Elsa's big bay head and led her out of her stall. Lynn called Dr. Hanson and within a half hour he was back feeding a tube through the old mare's nostril and into her stomach. He pumped a greasy mixture of glycerin and vegetable oil in and we waited to see if her stomach would settle or the blockage would pass. In a way it was nice to have Dr. Hanson back out there, even if Lynn was looking on with concerned eyes where I used to stand and I was in the place of Mom. He'd been our vet for a lot of years and run a lot of tubes down horses' nostrils. Not one for many words, he would sometimes surprise us with a wry comment. *Why do you always call me with bad news?* he might say, or *It's going to cost you extra if you want me to save him.* Sometimes his jokes fell flat, but we laughed all the same. He'd helped deliver foals and poultice legs and dress wounds and ease our old and sick out of this world with the grace and humanity of a man who's done it a million times. Even a sick horse was a welcome reminder of those days when Mom and Dad were home and the farm was still enough.

It was short lived though. *We caught it early,* he told us. *Just walk her for a little while and let the cramps settle. After that she can go out in the pasture. She should be fine.* And then Dr. Hanson packed up and was gone. The drama of the day had passed and Lynn went back to whatever she was doing. It was quiet again. The afternoon was creeping toward the hour when it always seemed to storm in the summer when we lived on the farm. The air took on a kind of static charge and the trees rustled a bit harder, more purposefully. I grabbed a rain jacket from the supply room and clipped a lead shank to Elsa's halter. *Let's go, old girl.*

We walked. Past the arena and the old geldings' field, behind the A-barn to the stretch of grass where the cow barn had stood when we first moved to the farm. Elsa ambled along steadily, the path of our steps as familiar to her as to me. Along the hedges Mom had planted as saplings and the spot by the house where the weeping willows had stood and both died within months of each other—one struck by lightning, the other rotted from inside. The sky was shifting, the colors deepening to a moody, plaintive grey. I could smell the rain before it began.

The pasture's iron gate squealed when I pulled it open, the rust from a thousand summer storms flaking at the hinges. *Go on,* I said to Elsa, unclipping the lead and patting her on the flank. She took a few steps, almost unsteady, like a newborn colt, and then found her footing and made her way into the heart of the field. The first of the rain began to *ping* off the iron gate and pelt the top of my head. I stood there and watched her. *Just you and me, Elsa. The only ones left.*

I saw her drop to her knees. Before I could get over the fence she had heaved herself to the ground and was rolling and thrashing—not the roll of an energetic yearling or a sweaty and itchy school horse, but the dreaded colic roll. *Come on, Elsa! Get up!* I barked at her, smacking at her rump. She wouldn't budge, and her rolling got more violent, her legs kicked out in all directions.

You don't realize how large a horse is until it no longer yields to your control and you see the massive tank of a belly and the muscles bulge beneath their coat. *Elsa! Stop!* I hollered, whipping at her with my rain jacket. A sound came from deep within the ocean of her, something primitive between a moan and a wail, something I'd never heard before. It was pouring by then, dumping on both of us, and the jacket was slippery in my hands, but I kept beating her with it, yelling at her to *Get up, get up, get up! Elsa, get up!* I saw a milky white substance come across her eyes, the elusive third eyelid only some animals have, that only some draw over their view in the last moments.

I should have known by then it was over, should have dropped my hands and let her pass, but I kept hitting her, kept screaming at her. I was unwilling to see that she was already gone, that everything was already over, that all things must pass, and that there is love that can be tested, that cannot be broken, that will answer the challenge and lie down in a field and die for another, and that there is life, still, in a girl who stands in the rain, beating down on a beast, saying *I'm not through yet. I'm still here.*

PROSTHESIS

Consider the problem of remembering names.

Pronounce one,
and you have already begun

to forget it, by law of sonic
condensation: gray matter raining

the excess from its fresh wash.
Consider adopting a crowd in your blood

that speaks an intravenous stream
of possible vowels,

a wheel-of-fortune spinning til it slows
on one of the poor pins of our alphabet.

After all, a man scans a clogged street for hours,
looking for the one who called him.

Consider a plastic bag snagged on a branch,
filled with a sour wind.

In some parts of the mouth, a drought.
At the river-bottom, carp's *ah* caught

on a piece of bark between its lips.
The first sound could be anything: plosive

between a knife's drawn tip
and fleshy palate. The hiss

as a lifeboat lowers into a watery grave.
Dynasty of babbling. The tongue's clamp and rig.

Consider the chances that these are the sounds
you will make in your sleep tonight.

JEN LEVITT

I Want to be Sincere Now

My worst nightmare is talking
on the phone for hours, my best
a Staten Island Ferry ride
or the time I joined an equestrian team,
jumping over fences, the ribboning meadow.
I wasn't scared though I'd never
touched a horse in this life.
In this life I want one microwaveable
meal, clear answer on a test,
a cloud chamber where I can listen
to the wind distort. My back
will be hooked to tubes charting
my progress as a human. I sleep stacked
among my books. How am I doing?

AMERICAN IDOL

I bought an electric toothbrush
because the dentist said I wasn't thorough enough
& wants to see me in two months.
The therapist prophesied a near-recovery,
predicted love would come eventually.
When the conductor asked for my ticket,
the reality was he'd been working
for ten hours straight & could use a smoke break,
but I had nothing to offer.

Now at night, I brush & brush to the whir
of the small machine, screen my calls,
put lettuce on tomorrow's sandwich.
I imagine I'm being interviewed
on a leather couch on a talk-show set
& when I tell a story about middle school
haircuts, everyone laughs. Outside, two teenagers
argue over video game graphics. On TV,
the finalists are forced to sing for their lives.

I/THEY

They amble until noticed. They point to familiar things in the room & this means whatever it does to them. Whose antagonist are you they ask. What arc does your anger trace. I hold my tongue in an effort to feel nameless. A man needs his heroes they say or why else would we hold you here. I am reminded of things as they looked in bad lighting. Was I the mistake or the motive. The fact in this instance is nothing remains sacred. Neither the heart nor its metonym. I wait with the others for some sense of an ending. They cite my deficiencies. You are waxmoon yellow they say. You're the unloved remainder. I set my teeth the task of deboning. The room makes amends with me. Our rituals I want to say determine our legacy. This feels Republican. This feels a little like stomaching glass for want of a window. If I am my best self am I merely mimetic. The mirror says yes. The mirror says no further questions.

BRADLEY HARRISON

THOUGH YOU LEFT ME I STILL WATER YOUR PLANTS

There are days I want to make you understand.
Days piled like a ship's splintered timbers
in a stockyard of the throat-slit moon.
There are days I want to call you
from the miles of my quiet to tell you
how she wore the same panties
you would sometimes wear. How with nerves
I worked my mouth down her frame,
hands rubbing for warmth,
to maybe catch a spark,
her opened jeans I pulled away
and saw them there in cotton,
the horizontal stripes and lacy trim,
gray and white and everything
left me when you did. But these. You left me
these. I am no werewolf but
I took them all the same in my teeth
and I tore you open gently, that I might
find myself in you again, get lost in the trees
with your lit match in my mouth.

CONTRIBUTOR'S NOTES

JAMES TADD ADCOX is the author of *The Map of the System of Human Knowledge* (Tiny Hardcore Press, 2012) and a novel, *Does Not Love* (Curbside Splendor Press, forthcoming 2014). He lives in Chicago.

KIRSTIN ALLIO's novel, *Garner* (Coffee House), was a finalist for the LA Times Book Prize for First Fiction. She has received the National Book Foundation's "5 Under 35" Award, a PEN/O. Henry prize, and has published short stories, and a novella, in many journals.

JOHN R. BEARDSLEY divides his time between Evansville, Indiana, where he teaches Composition at the University of Southern Indiana, and Tallahassee, Florida, where he is pursuing a doctorate in Creative Writing at Florida State University. His poems have recently appeared or are forthcoming in *The Journal, Third Coast, American Literary Review*, and *Makeout Creek*.

LEIGH BENNETT teaches composition to unsuspecting undergrads in Boston where she breathes and writes. She holds a BA from Wellesley College and an MA in English and American Literature from Boston University. She is an MFA candidate at Bennington College.

DMITRY BORSHCH was born in Dnepropetrovsk, studied in Moscow, and today lives in New York. His paintings have been exhibited at the National Arts Club (New York), Brecht Forum (New York), ISE Cultural Foundation (New York), the State Russian Museum (Saint Petersburg).

HISHAM BUSTANI has three published collections of short fiction in Arabic, and is acclaimed for his contemporary themes, style, and language. His translated stories have appeared in *The Saint Ann's Review, The Common*, and *World Literature Today*. He was recently listed by *The Culture Trip* website as one of the six best contemporary writers in Jordan.

JUSTIN CARROLL was born in California and raised in Montana. He has an MFA from Texas State University and is an assistant editor for the Austin-based literary journal *Unstuck*. His work has been previously published in *Juked* and *Gulf Coast*.

JAMES D'AGOSTINO is the author of *Nude With Anything* (New Issues Press) and *Slur Oeuvre* (New Michigan Press). He directs the BFA program in creative writing at Truman State University.

ALLISON DAVIS is the author of *Poppy Seeds* (KSU Press, 2013). Born and raised in Youngstown, Ohio, she lives in California where she is a Wallace Stegner Fellow at Stanford University.

CODY ERNST's work has appeared in *Word Riot*. He is currently pursuing an MFA in The Writing Seminars at Johns Hopkins University.

LEAH FALK is from Pittsburgh. Her poems can be found in issues of *Kenyon Review*, *Smartish Pace*, *FIELD* and other journals. She is at work on a collection of poems about the life and ideas of Alan Turing.

LEORA FRIDMAN is the author of "Precious Coast" (H_ngm_n B_ _ks), "On the architecture" and "Essential Nature" (The New Megaphone), and "Eduardo Milán: Poems" (Toad Press). With Kelin Loe, she edits *Spoke Too Soon: A Journal of the Longer*.

JASON GORDON was born and raised in Baltimore, Maryland. His work has appeared in *Amethyst Arsenic*, *Cleaver*, *Poetry International*, *Presa*, and *Weave*, among others. He currently lives in Catonsville, Maryland, teaching English at a middle school for dyslexic children.

ANNIE GUTHRIE is a writer and jeweler living in Tucson. Her book *the good dark* is forthcoming from Tupelo Press. She teaches Oracular Writing at the University of Arizona Poetry Center.

BRADLEY HARRISON is a graduate of the Michener Center for Writers at the University of Texas in Austin. His work can be found in *New American Writing*, *Forklift Ohio*, *West Branch*, *Best New Poets 2012* and elsewhere. His chapbook *Diorama of a People, Burning* is available from Ricochet Editions (2012). He currently teaches at Truman State University.

VEDRAN HUSIĆ was born in Mostar, Bosnia and Herzegovina. His fiction is published in *Witness, North American Review, The Massachusetts Review,* and elsewhere. Currently, he is a Writing Fellow at the Fine Arts Work Center in Provincetown, Massachusetts.

HANAE JONAS lives in Vermont. Other poems have appeared or are forthcoming in *Handsome* and *DIAGRAM*.

BECCA KLAVER is the author of the poetry collection *LA Liminal* (Kore Press, 2010) and several chapbooks, including *Nonstop Pop* (Bloof Books, 2013) and *Merrily, Merrily* (Lame House Press, 2013). She is a PhD candidate in English at Rutgers University and lives in Brooklyn, NY.

KEEGAN LESTER's poems have been published in or are forthcoming from: *The Barn Owl Review, Ilk Journal, Sixth Finch, Moon City Review* and *Death Hums,* among others. He is a cofounder of the journal *Souvenir* and lives in Morgantown, West Virginia.

JEN LEVITT received her MFA from NYU. She lives in New York City and teaches high school students.

EMILY HO is an MFA graduate from Brigham Young University. Her work has appeared or is forthcoming in *Pleiades, Anti-, Booth,* and elsewhere. She's also the recipient of an Academy of American Poets prize, and a Hart-Larsen poetry prize.

KELLY MOFFETT's collection, *A Thousand Black Wings,* will be out February 2014 through Salmon Poetry. Her work has appeared in journals such as *Colorado Review, Redactions, Cincinnati Review* and *Rattle.* She teaches poetry at Northern Kentucky University.

NAOMI MULVIHILL is currently a fellow at the Fine Arts Work Center in Provincetown. Her poems have appeared or are forthcoming in *Iron Horse Literary Review, New Orleans Review, Cave Wall* and others.

CHRISTINA OLSON is the author of a book of poems, *Before I Came Home Naked*. Recent writing has appeared, or is forthcoming, in *The Southern Review*, *River Styx*, *Gastronomica*, *Nimrod*, and *Salamander*. She is the poetry editor of *Midwestern Gothic*, and lives both in Georgia and online at www.thedrevlow-olsonshow.com.

JODY RAMBO's first collection, *Tethering World*, was published in 2011 by The Kent State UP. Her poems have appeared in *Barrow Street*, *Colorado Review*, *Gulf Coast*, *Virginia Quarterly Review*, and others. She lives in Springfield, Ohio, where she teaches at Wittenberg University.

ANNA REESER is an illustrator, writer and graphic designer in Seattle, WA. Her work has appeared in *The Destroyer*, *The Suisun Valley Review* and *The Nervous Breakdown*. Born and raised in a southern California chaparral valley, Anna has been moving north—first to Berkeley where she studied creative writing and printmaking, then to Seattle where she now lives with her boyfriend and cat. She loves hiking up mountains and bicycling around cities, especially at night.

SEAN RYS lives in Tucson, Arizona, where he teaches composition and creative writing at the University of Arizona. His work has previously appeared or is forthcoming in the journals *elimae*, *DIAGRAM*, *Indiana Review*, *The International Literary Quarterly* and *Devil's Lake*.

LIV STRATMAN is an MFA candidate at the University of Wisconsin-Madison, where she won the 2013 David and Jean Milofsky Prize for fiction. She divides the year between Madison and her native New York.

JACOB SUNDERLIN received an MFA from Purdue University and a poetry fellowship from the Fine Arts Work Center in Provincetown, MA. His work appears or is forthcoming in *Colorado Review*, *Cream City Review*, *Ploughshares*, and elsewhere.

DEVON TAYLOR received her MFA in creative nonfiction from the University of Memphis. Her work has appeared in the *Tottenville Review* and *Plaid Horse*. She lives in Memphis, Tennessee, where she collects stray dogs and dreams of mountains.

SAM THAYN is an MFA student in Creative Writing at Brigham Young University in Utah. His work has been published in *Inscape: A Journal of Literature and Art*, and *likewise folio*. He is currently working on a chapbook entitled *The Disasters*.

AMISH TRIVEDI's poems can be found in *Mandorla*, *XCP*, *Esque*, *Omni-Verse*, *Noö* and forthcoming in *New American Writing*. Reviews, etc. are on *Jacket2*, *ColdFront*, and *Octopus*. He is the managing editor of *N/A* and can be found at www.amishtrivedi.com

SARAH VALLANCE recently completed an MFA in Creative Non-Fiction at City University in Hong Kong. She has a story forthcoming in the *Gettysburg Review* and is in the final stages of editing her memoir.

BRAD VOGLER's poems have appeared in places which include: *Dear Sir, Versal*, *Barzakh*, and *Word for/Word*, and he has work forthcoming in *Volt, Jacket2* and *Bestoned*. He builds and maintains the website for Delete Press (www.delete-press.org), and is the editor/web designer of *Opon* (www.opon.org). His first chapbook, *Fascicle 30*, was published by Little Red Leaves Textile Series.

DILLON J. WELCH is a writer from Southern New Hampshire. His work has appeared in *Gargoyle*, *ILK*, *PANK*, *Switchback*, and other journals. He is Poetry Co-Editor for the online quarterly, *Swarm*. Find him at: ratrapss.tumblr.com

DEREK JG WILLIAMS is an MFA candidate at UMass Boston. His poems and prose are published or forthcoming in *Best New Poets 2013*, *Bellingham Review*, *H_NGM_N*, *Knockout*, *Nailed Magazine*, and *LUMINA*, among others.

SHELLEY WONG is a Kundiman fellow and a poetry editor for The Journal. Her poetry has appeared or is forthcoming in *Nashville Review*, *The Adroit Journal*, *Lantern Review*, and *Linebreak*.

山寨
PACIFICA LITERARY REVIEW

CALL FOR SUBMISSIONS

Like many things in America today, the concept of shanzhai (山寨) is imported from China. Literally, 山寨 means "mountain stronghold," where bandits and outlaws lived and did as they pleased outside the control and reach of a corrupt central government. From that context, 山寨 has evolved to describe everything from knockoff products and fly-by-night enterprises to jury-rigged devices and Chairman Mao impersonators. Novelist Yu Hua, writing of 山寨 in his 2011 book *China in Ten Words*, says:

> ...the word [山寨] has given the word 'imitation' a new meaning...allowing it to acquire additional shades of meaning: counterfeiting, infringement, deviations from the standard, mischief, and caricature.

山寨 straddles the line between innovative design and shameless thievery, clever parody and outright mockery, between freedom from authority and the social threat that freedom represents. Every time we examine our lives and the things in it to determine what is authentic, and what is cheap imitation, we implicitly acknowledge that 山寨 is real, and that it matters. There's something threatening in the thought that much of what we construct ourselves of (and as) could be fake somehow, a rip-off of what we really want, some manufacturer's idea of what we should be. We feel duped, tricked, lessened; we were promised some articulation of self and instead got an artikulatun. There's also something liberating in the thought that perhaps the materials we've made ourselves of are unsanctioned, wildly inventive in the way they suit our particular needs, and slyly subversive. We feel vindicated, emboldened, alive; we assembled, from the detritus of the world, a self that is unique and ungovernable. **PACIFICA LITERARY REVIEW** seeks writing, art, and photography that engages with 山寨, that which examines what's real and what's counterfeit, what's reimagining and what's theft, what's art and what's artifice, and how much of each is in everything we do.

www.pacificareview.com